BASIC DUTCH:
A GRAMMAR AND WORKBOOK

Basic Dutch: A Grammar and Workbook comprises an accessible reference grammar and related exercises in a single volume.

This workbook presents 25 individual grammar points in realistic contexts, providing a grammatical approach which will allow students not already familiar with these structures to become accustomed to their use. Grammar points are followed by examples and exercises designed to reinforce and consolidate students' learning.

Suitable for class use or self-study, *Basic Dutch* introduces Dutch culture and people through the medium of the language used today, providing students with the basic tools to express themselves in a wide variety of situations.

Features include:

- useful exercises and full answer key
- grammar tables for easy reference
- frequent comparative references to English grammar
- appendix of irregular verbs
- index of grammatical terms.

Jenneke A. Oosterhoff is Senior Lecturer in the Department of German, Scandinavian and Dutch at the University of Minnesota.

Other titles available in the Grammar Workbooks series are:

Basic Cantonese
Intermediate Cantonese

Basic Chinese
Intermediate Chinese

Intermediate Dutch

Basic German
Intermediate German

Basic Irish
Intermediate Irish

Basic Italian

Basic Korean
Intermediate Korean
(forthcoming)

Basic Polish
Intermediate Polish

Basic Russian
Intermediate Russian

Basic Spanish
Intermediate Spanish

Basic Welsh
Intermediate Welsh

BASIC DUTCH: A GRAMMAR AND WORKBOOK

Jenneke A. Oosterhoff

Illustrated by Ari Hoptman

Routledge
Taylor & Francis Group

LONDON AND NEW YORK

First published 2009
by Routledge
2 Park Square, Milton Park, Abingdon, Oxon OX14 4RN

Simultaneously published in the USA and Canada
by Routledge
711 Third Avenue, New York, NY 10017

Routledge is an imprint of the Taylor & Francis Group, an informa business

© 2009 Jenneke A. Oosterhoff

Typeset in Times Ten by Graphicraft Limited, Hong Kong

British Library Cataloguing in Publication Data
A catalogue record for this book is available from the British Library

Library of Congress Cataloging-in-Publication Data
Oosterhoff, Jenneke.
   Basic Dutch : a grammar and workbook / Jenneke Oosterhoff.
      p. cm.
   Includes index.
   1. Dutch language—Grammar.   2. Dutch language—Textbooks for foreign
speakers—English.   I. Title.
PF112
439.31—dc22

2008032503

ISBN10: 0–415–48488–X (hbk)
ISBN10: 0–415–77443–8 (pbk)
ISBN10: 0–203–88310–1 (ebk)

ISBN13: 978–0–415–48488–6 (hbk)
ISBN13: 978–0–415–77443–7 (pbk)
ISBN13: 978–0–203–88310–5 (ebk)

CONTENTS

Contents

PREFACE

This book is a basic Dutch reference grammar with exercises for absolute beginners or learners who want to refine their knowledge of grammatical structures. Each unit presents a grammatical topic with an introduction and where necessary an overview in a table, followed by clear and concise explanations in English and ending with a series of contextualized exercises. The explanations are illustrated by examples in Dutch, and some images are included to provide a more humorous context.

This basic grammar workbook is suitable for independent learning as well as for classroom use. Its contents cover the materials typical for first-year curriculum Dutch as a foreign language taught at university level. Using vocabulary associated with topics featured in typical first-year Dutch language textbooks, it can accompany any such textbook used in classroom language instruction.

This is strictly a grammar book. It doesn't include a chapter on pronunciation, because the internet provides numerous examples on this topic, including audio files. This book, however, provides clear explanations of grammatical terms, contrasted with examples in English, and it gives special attention to grammatical aspects of spelling.

Language is best learned and practiced in context. Sample sentences and exercises in traditional grammar books often lack such context. Most examples and exercises in this book, however, are written in context, using an imaginary Dutch family of four and their circle of friends and neighbors to provide a situational context. The exercises teach the learner to first recognize the grammar structure and then apply it in more complex forms. For classroom purposes, some speaking exercises suitable for group work are also included. For immediate feedback, a key to the exercises is provided at the back of this book.

For help in writing this grammar workbook, I have consulted many excellent reference grammars and other Dutch grammar workbooks, first and foremost the *Algemene Nederlandse Spraakkunst* (Martinus Nijhoff, 1997), but also works such as *Dutch: An Essential Grammar* (Routledge, 2002), *De Regels van het Nederlands* (Wolters Noordhoff, 1994) and *Nederlandse Grammatica voor Anderstaligen* (Utrecht, 1985). I am indebted to the people at taaladvies.net for sending me quick and helpful answers to complex grammatical questions. I specially thank Wijnie de Groot and Alice van Kalsbeek for constructive comments and moral support along the way, and I am most grateful to my students Heidi Raatz and Julia Belgum for proofreading my chapters and asking me exactly the right questions. Many thanks also to Ari Hoptman for providing the images to underline the grammar with good laughs, and, lastly, I want to thank the College of Liberal Arts at the University of Minnesota for granting me a leave of absence to finish this project.

Jenneke A. Oosterhoff
St. Paul, July 2008

Further Reading

A. Florijn, J. Lalleman, H. Maureau (1994) *De Regels van het Nederlands.* Groningen: Wolters-Noordhoff.

A. M. Fontein, A. Pescher-ter Meer (1985) *Nederlandse Grammatica voor Anderstaligen.* Utrecht: Nederlands Centrum Buitenlanders.

W. Hasereyn, K. Romijn, G. Geerts, J. de Rooij, M. C. van den Toorn (1997) *Algemene Nederlandse Spraakkunst.* Groningen: Martinus Nijhoff.

W. Z. Shetter, I. van der Cruysse-Van Antwerpen (2002) *Dutch: An Essential Grammar.* London and New York: Routledge.

UNIT ONE
Verbs and pronouns

Introduction

Two basic elements of a grammatical sentence are a subject and a verb:
Ik ga 'I go', **Jij eet** 'You eat', **Peter werkt** 'Peter works', **We spelen** 'We play'. This first chapter, therefore, is an introduction to the subject forms of the personal pronoun and verbs in the present tense.

The chapter includes a section on spelling in verb conjugation.

Subject forms of the personal pronoun: overview

Singular

1st person	**ik**	I
2nd person	**jij/je** (informal), **u** (formal)	you
3rd person	**hij** (masculine), **zij/ze** (feminine), **het** (neuter)	he, she, it

Plural

1st person	**wij/we**	we
2nd person	**jullie** (informal), **u** (formal, verb in singular)	you
3rd person	**zij/ze**	they

Notes and examples

1 Personal pronouns refer to both persons and things. A person might be introduced by his or her name, and further statements about that person begin with the personal pronoun that corresponds in gender and number. See the following examples:

> **Henk woont in Zeist.** *Hij* **werkt in Utrecht.**
> Henk lives in Zeist. *He* works in Utrecht.

Maria is lerares. *Ze* werkt part-time.
Maria is a teacher. *She* works part-time.

In reference to objects, the subject pronoun **het** is used for nouns in the singular which are neuter (**het**-words), **hij** is used for nouns in the singular which are masculine and feminine (**de**-words), and **zij**, **ze** is used for nouns in the plural. Note: The Dutch almost never refer to an object using the feminine personal pronoun **zij**, **ze**, as is often done in English, for example when the car mechanic says to the customer: "I took your car for a spin, and she works fine now." Commonly, in Dutch we use the subject pronoun **hij** or **het** where English would use it. Examples:

Waar is het boek? *Het* zit in mijn tas.
Where is the book? It's in my bag.

Hoe oud is je huis? *Het* is 80 jaar oud.
How old is your house? It is 80 years old.

Hoe vind je de vis? *Hij* smaakt lekker.
How do you like the fish? It tastes good.

Wat kosten de noten? *Ze* kosten een euro.
How much are the nuts? They're one euro.

2 Some of the pronouns have stressed and unstressed forms, such as **jij** versus **je** in the second person singular, and **zij** versus **ze** in the third person singular feminine and in the third person plural, and **wij** versus **we** in the first person plural. Whether you use the stressed or the unstressed form depends on where you place the emphasis in the (spoken) sentence. Examples:

a **Ik woon in Olst. Waar woon *jij*?** I live in Olst. Where do *you* live?
b **Woon je *ook* in Olst?** Do you *also* live in Olst?
c **Hoe heet *zij*?** What is *her* name?
d **En waar *woont* ze?** And where does she *live*?

In example a, the emphasis is on **jij** in order to distinguish from **ik**. In b, the second person has been introduced, and the emphasis can be placed on something else, in this case **ook**. The same principle is at work in examples c and d. The subject is introduced with emphasis in c, and in d it is not the subject, but the verb that is stressed.

3 In Dutch we distinguish between the informal form for the second person singular, **jij** or **je**, and the formal **u**. In the second person plural, we use informal **jullie** versus formal **u**. While the informal **jij**, **je**, and **jullie** are becoming more and more commonplace in everyday speech, the formal **u** is still widely used as a polite form in interactions among people from different generations (although parents and children, and even grandparents and grandchildren often use **jij**, **je**, and **jullie**),

people who don't know each other such as store or office personnel and customers, and people in different hierarchical positions or ranks. Addressing someone as **meneer** or **mevrouw** or with a formal title, one must use **u**. In formal letters, one must always use **u**.

Examples of formal speech: To ask a stranger who looks older than 18 for directions, you might say: "**Pardon, mag ik *u* iets vragen? Weet *u* waar het station is?**" "Pardon me, may I ask you something? Do you know where the station is?" In a store, the owner or store personnel will probably say to you: "**Kan ik *u* helpen?**" "Can I help you?" A waiter in a restaurant may approach you saying: "**Zegt *u* het maar**" (literally "Please say it"). This would be the equivalent of "May I take your order?" If you ring someone's doorbell to ask for money for a charity organization, and it is raining cats and dogs outside, the person opening the door may say to you: "**Komt *u* maar even binnen**" "Please step inside for a moment."

4 There are also unstressed forms of **ik**, **hij**, and **het**: **'k**, **-ie** (always following the verb), **'t**. You will hear them in speech or see them in written (often literary) texts. Examples:

a **'k Heb geen tijd.** (= **Ik heb geen tijd.**) I have no time.
b **Wat zegt-*ie*?** (= **Wat zegt hij?**) What is he saying?
c **'t Is een goed boek.** (= **Het is een goed boek.**) It's a good book.

Exercise 1.1

Put the correct personal pronoun under each image.

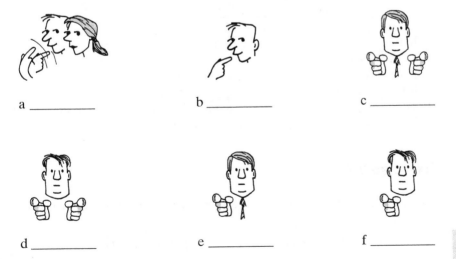

a _____

b _____

c _____

d _____

e _____

f _____

g _____   h _____

Exercise 1.2

Enter the correct form of the subject pronoun.

Situation: Karin introduces herself, her family, her best friend.

Hoi, _____ (1) ben Karin Beumer. Mijn vader heet Erik, _____ (2) is advocaat, _____ (3) werkt voor een verzekeringsbank. Mijn moeder heet Sanne, _____ (4) is lerares en _____ (5) werkt parttime op een basisschool. Ik heb een broer, _____ (6) heet Peter. _____ (7) wonen in Hardegarijp, een dorp in Friesland. Opa en oma Beumer komen uit Groningen, maar _____ (8) wonen nu in Leeuwarden. Dan heb ik nog opa en oma Hulst. _____ (9) wonen in Leiden. Mijn beste vriendin heet Petra. _____ (10) doen alles samen. Willen _____ (11) een paar foto's zien?

Exercise 1.3

Enter the correct form of the subject pronoun. The dialogue is informal.

Situation: Karin meets a new friend at school.

1 Ina: Hoi, hoe heet _____?
2 Karin: _____ heet Karin. En _____?
3 Ina: _____ ben Ina. Woon _____ in Sneek?
4 Karin: Nee, in Hardegarijp. _____ kom met de bus naar school.
5 Ina: Heb _____ broers en zussen?
6 Karin: Ja, een broer, Peter. _____ zit in 5 HAVO. En _____?
7 Ina: _____ heb een zus. _____ zit nog op de basisschool.
8 Karin: Kom, _____ gaan naar binnen.

Exercise 1.4

Enter the correct form of the subject pronoun. Parts of the dialogue are formal.

Situation: In the classroom. After class, the students go to the school canteen.

1 Karin: Meneer Kampen, kunt _____ me even helpen?

2 Oscar: Meneer Kampen, moeten _____ oefening ('exercise') 8 ook doen?

3 Hans: Hé Oscar, weet _____ het huiswerk voor morgen?

4 Joris: Meneer Kampen, heeft _____ de proefwerken ('tests') van gisteren?

5 Oscar: Jongens, _____ gaan koffie drinken. Gaan _____ mee?

6 Ina: Wacht even. Karin is naar de wc. _____ komt zo.

7 Karin: Hier ben _____ . Waar zijn de anderen?

8 Ina: _____ zijn al in de kantine. Kom _____?

Exercise 1.5

Answer Erik's questions using the subject form of the personal pronoun. Remember to use **hij** to refer to **de-** words in the singular.

Situation: Erik comes home. He can't find anything. He's looking for his paper, his house shoes, his coffee, his kids. Sanne, who is in the kitchen, has all the answers.

Erik
1 Waar is de krant?
2 Waar zijn m'n pantoffels?
3 Sanne, waar ben jij?
4 Waar staat m'n koffie?
5 Waar zijn de kinderen?
6 Is het eten al klaar?
7 Wat doen jij en Jolanda vanavond?
8 Hoe is die nieuwe trainer?

Sanne
_____ ligt op de tafel.
_____ staan onder het bed.
_____ ben in de keuken.
_____ staat hier in de keuken.
_____ maken huiswerk.
_____ is om zes uur klaar, Erik!
_____ gaan naar de sportschool.
_____ is goed. En heel aardig.

Verb conjugation in the present tense

The verb is the part in the sentence that indicates what the subject does, how it changes, what condition or (mental) state it is in, what happens to it, where it goes, etc. Examples:

Erik *woont* in Hardegarijp. Hij *werkt* in Leeuwarden. Hij *is* advocaat. Hij *is* getrouwd. Hij *heeft* twee kinderen. Ze *heten* Peter en Karin. Peter en Karin *gaan* naar de middelbare school.
Erik lives in Hardegarijp. He works in Leeuwarden. He is a lawyer. He is married. He has two children. Their names are Peter and Karin. Peter and Karin go to high school.

The verb corresponds with its subject in person and number. In the sentence **Erik woont in Hardegarijp**, the subject (**Erik**) is third person singular. In the sentence **Peter en Karin gaan naar de middelbare school**, the subject (**Peter en Karin**) is third person plural. Subject–verb agreement is accomplished with verb endings.

Examples and notes

werken[1]

	Singular		Plural
ik	werk	**wij/we**	werk*en*
jij/je	werk*t* / werk je[2]	**jullie**	werk*en*
u	werk*t*	**u**	werk*t*[3]
hij, zij/ze, het	werk*t*	**zij/ze**	werk*en*

1 **Werken** is the infinitive, the non-conjugated form of the verb, as it appears in the dictionary. In English, the infinitive begins with 'to': to work, to live, to play. In most verbs, the infinitive consists of a stem (**werk-**) and the ending **-en**. When conjugated in a sentence, the stem loses the ending **-en**, which is replaced by the appropriate verb ending (italic in the table). The verb form for **ik** is the same as the stem.

2 When **jij** or **je** follow the verb, the ending **-t** is dropped. This happens, for instance, in questions or when something other than the subject takes the first place in the sentence.

> *Werk* **je in een restaurant?**   Do you work in a restaurant?
> *Maak* **jij nu je huiswerk?**   Are you doing your homework now?

3 The verb ending for formal **u** is always **-t**, whether it is singular or plural.

The verbs hebben (to have) and zijn (to be)

	hebben		**zijn**
ik	*heb*	**ik**	*ben*
jij/je	*hebt (heb je/jij)*	**jij/je**	*bent (ben je/jij)*
u	*hebt/heeft*	**u**	*bent*
hij, zij/ze, het	*heeft*	**hij, zij/ze, het**	*is*
wij/we	*hebben*	**wij/we**	*zijn*
jullie	*hebben*	**jullie**	*zijn*
zij/ze	*hebben*	**zij/ze**	*zijn*

Verbs with stems that end in -t or -d

Some verb stems end in **-t** or **-d**. In verbs with a stem ending in **-t**, we *do not* add the verb ending **-t** in the second and third person singular. In verbs with a stem ending in **-d**, we *do* add a **-t** to the second and third person singular. In the inverted form in the second person singular, some of these verbs drop the **-d**. See examples in the singular:

	zetten put	**weten** know	**houden** hold	**raden** guess
ik	zet	weet	houd	raad
jij/je	zet/zet je	weet/weet je	houdt/hou(d) je	raadt/raad je
u	zet	weet	houdt	raadt
hij, zij/ze, het	zet	weet	houdt	raadt

Some unusual infinitives

Of some frequently used, one-syllable verbs, the stem ends in **-n** instead of **-en**. The table below shows how they are conjugated in singular and plural.

		gaan go	**zien** see	**doen** do
Singular	**ik**	ga	zie	doe
	jij/je, u	gaat/ga je	ziet/zie je	doet/doe je
	hij, zij/ze, het	gaat	ziet	doet
Plural	**wij/we, jullie, zij/ze**	gaan	zien	doen

Note: **slaan** 'hit' and **staan** 'stand' follow the same pattern as **gaan**.

Spelling in verb conjugation

Note the difference between the verbs **spelen** 'to play' and **spellen** 'to spell' in conjugation in singular and plural. For simplification, the personal pronouns have been omitted from these (and the following) examples.

spelen		**spellen**	
speel[1]	spelen	spel[2]	spellen
speelt (speel je)	spelen	spelt (spel je)	spellen
speelt	spelen	spelt	spellen

1 In Dutch, spelling is determined largely by the way words are divided into syllables, and whether syllables are open or closed. The verb **spelen** is divided as follows: **spe-len**, the word is split after the vowel

and before the single consonant. The syllable **spe-** is open. The verb **spellen** is divided as follows: **spel-len**, the word is split between the double consonant. The syllable **spel-** is closed. An open syllable ends in a vowel; a closed syllable ends in a consonant. A single vowel in an open syllable (**spe-**) is pronounced long, a single vowel in a closed syllable (**spel-**) is pronounced short. In order to keep the vowel in **spelen** long within a closed syllable (**speel**), we have to double it. Here, proper pronunciation and spelling of a word is very important. If spelled or pronounced incorrectly, the meaning of the word can change. If we didn't double the vowel of **spelen** in first, second, and third person singular, it would be pronounced the same as in the verb **spellen**. Note: the verb **komen** (**ik kom**) is an exception to this rule.

2 Closed syllables in Dutch (**spel-**) never end in two identical consonants. Furthermore, two identical consonants are never followed by a single consonant (**spellt**). Therefore, the double consonant in **spellen** is reduced to one in the first, second, and third person singular. In the plural, surrounded by vowels, it is once again double. See more examples of these basic spelling rules in the following table. Each time, a verb with a long vowel is contrasted with a verb with a short vowel. Only the infinitive and first person singular and plural are given. The verbs are **wonen** 'to live', **winnen** 'to win', **spreken** 'to speak', **trekken** 'to pull', **laten** 'to let', **zitten** 'to sit'.

wonen	winnen	spreken	trekken	laten	zitten
ik woon	ik win	ik spreek	ik trek	ik laat	ik zit
wij wonen	wij winnen	wij spreken	wij trekken	wij laten	wij zitten

In Dutch, **v** and **z** cannot be at the end of a syllable, and are 'hardened' (voiceless) in front of another hard consonant. Therefore, in first, second, and third person singular, **v** turns into **f** and **z** turns into **s**. Note the differences in spelling in singular and plural in the verbs **geven** 'to give' and **wijzen** 'to point'.

geven		wijzen	
geef	geven	wijs	wijzen
geeft (geef je)	geven	wijst (wijs je)	wijzen
geeft	geven	wijst	wijzen

Exercise 1.6

To practice correct spelling, enter the first person singular and the first person plural in the table.

1 vragen	2 zeggen	3 nemen	4 zwemmen	5 leven
ik	ik	ik	ik	ik
wij	wij	wij	wij	wij

6 reizen	7 hebben	8 lopen	9 zitten	10 laten
ik	ik	ik	ik	ik
wij	wij	wij	wij	wij

Exercise 1.7

Enter the correct verb forms into the table.

	1 kopen	2 passen	3 eten	4 schrijven	5 lezen
ik					
jij/je, u					
	je	je	je	je	je
hij, zij/ze, het					
wij/we					
jullie					
zij/ze					

Exercise 1.8

Jij ook? In the following exercise, enter the correct verb form in the second person singular.

1 Ik ga naar Amsterdam. _____ je mee?
2 Ik koop in Amsterdam een souvenir. _____ je ook een souvenir?
3 Ik drink op een terras een kopje koffie. _____ je ook een kopje?
4 Ik bezoek het Rijksmuseum. _____ je het museum ook?
5 Ik eet 's avonds op het Leidseplein een pizza. _____ je ook een pizza?

Exercise 1.9

Enter the correct forms of **hebben** and **zijn**.

Situation: Peter talks about his family.

Hoi, ik _____ (1) Peter, en dit _____ (2) mijn familie. Ik _____ (3) geen broers, maar wel een zus, Karin. Mijn vader

_____ (4) advocaat, mijn moeder _____ (5) lerares. Karin en ik _____ (6) vier grootouders, opa en oma Beumer en opa en oma Hulst. Mijn vader _____ (7) geen broers en zussen, maar ik _____ (8) wel tantes en ooms van mijn moeders kant, want zij _____ (9) een grote familie. Een keer per jaar _____ (10) we met de hele familie bij opa en oma Hulst voor de grote jaarlijkse reünie. Dat _____ (11) altijd heel leuk. En jij? _____ (12) je een grote familie?

Exercise 1.10

For each blank, choose the right verb and enter the correct form. Select from: **wonen, werken, komen, zijn, heten, spellen, gaan, studeren**.

Situation: Meet Hanife!

Dag! Mijn naam _____ (1) Hanife. Dat _____ (2) je H-A-N-I-F-E. Ik _____ (3) uit Turkije, maar ik _____ (4) in Nederland. Ik _____ (5) aan de Vrije Universiteit in Amsterdam. Ik _____ (6) op vrijdag- en zaterdagavond in een restaurant. Mijn beste vriendin _____ (7) Linda. Zij _____ (8) ook in dat restaurant. Maar zij _____ (9) in Alkmaar. Ze _____ (10) elke dag met de trein naar Amsterdam. Volgende week _____ (11) we samen op vakantie naar Spanje. En wie _____ (12) jij? _____ (13) je uit Nederland? Waar _____ (14) je? Wat _____ (15) je van beroep? Of _____ (16) je student?

Exercise 1.11

Conjugate the verbs correctly in the third person singular.

Situation: Erik is at the market.

Erik (zijn) _____ (1) op de markt. Hij (kopen) _____ (2) een kilo appels. Hij (vragen) _____ (3): "Wat kosten de bananen?" Hij (nemen) _____ (4) twee kilo bananen. Hij (betalen) _____ (5) met 100 euro. Hij (hebben) _____ (6) geen kleingeld. Erik (gaan) _____ (7) ook naar de kaasboer. Hij (zeggen) _____ (8): "Een stuk oude kaas, graag." De verkoper (wegen) _____ (9) een groot stuk kaas. Erik (vinden) _____ (10) het stuk te groot. De verkoper (snijden) _____ (11) een kleiner stuk. "Dat (zijn) _____ (12) goed."

UNIT TWO
Modal auxiliary verbs

Introduction

Modal verbs, also called modal auxiliary (helping) verbs, can change the
mood of the main verb in the sentence by expressing modalities such as
possibility (**kunnen** 'can'), necessity (**moeten** 'must', 'have to'), permission
(**mogen** 'may'), volition (**willen** 'want'), and recommendation (**zullen**
'should').

Conjugation of five modal verbs

	kunnen	**moeten**	**mogen**	**willen**	**zullen**
ik	kan	moet	mag	wil	zal
jij/je, u	kunt/kan	moet	mag	wilt	zult/zal
	kun/kan je	moet je	mag je	wil je	zul/zal je
hij, zij/ze, het	*kan*	*moet*	*mag*	*wil*	*zal*
wij/we	kunnen	moeten	mogen	willen	zullen
jullie	kunnen	moeten	mogen	willen	zullen
zij/ze	kunnen	moeten	mogen	willen	zullen

In a sentence in the present tense, the modal verb takes the position of
the conjugated verb, while the main verb, now in its *infinitive* form, moves
to the end of the sentence.

Wilt **u iets drinken?**	Would you like to drink something?
Kunt **u mij even helpen?**	Can you help me for a minute?
Erik *moet* **vanavond werken.**	Erik has to work tonight.
Zullen **we naar de bioscoop gaan?**	Shall we go to the movies?

U *mag* hier niet roken.   You may not smoke here.

The following examples demonstrate the difference in meaning:

***Kun* je komen? *Kan* je komen?**	Can you, are you able to come?
***Moet* je komen?**	Must you, do you have to come?
***Wil* je komen?**	Do you want to come?
***Zul* je komen? *Zal* je komen?**	Will you, shall you come?
***Mag* je komen?**	May you, are you allowed to come?

Note: English speaking students of Dutch easily confuse **willen** and **zullen**. The verb **willen** means want to, not will! **Ik wil** = I want, **Ik zal** = I will.

Sometimes, the main or action verb infinitive at the end of the sentence is left out. It is, however, implied. Note the following examples:

Kom je vanavond? Nee, ik *kan* niet. The verb **komen** is implied.
Are you coming tonight? No, I can't (come).

Moet ik dit boek lezen? Ja, dat *moet*. The words **je lezen** are implied.
Do I have to read this book? Yes, you must (read it).

Eet je je broodje op? Nee, ik *wil* niet. The verb **eten** is implied.
Are you eating your sandwich? No, I don't want to (eat it).

Mag ik hier parkeren? Ja, dat *mag*. The words **je/u doen** are implied.
May I park here? Yes, you may (park here).

The verbs **mogen** and **moeten** often appear with the preposition **van**. The preposition expresses who gives the permission or command to do what is expressed in the main verb. Examples:

Ik mag *van* mijn vader niet roken.	My father doesn't allow me to smoke.
***Van* mij mag je die broek wel kopen.**	I allow you to buy those pants.

Van wie moeten we dat doen?   Who says we have to do that?
Ik moet *van* m'n moeder thuisblijven.   My mom tells me to stay
home.

This concludes the introduction to modal auxiliary verbs. We will return
to the topic of verbs with infinitives in Unit 22.

Exercise 2.1

Add the modal verb to the sentence.
   Example: Kom je vanavond? (kunnen) ⇒ *Kun* je vanavond komen?

   Situation: Erik is helping Sanne with some chores around the house.

1 Sanne: Erik, zet je het vuilnis buiten? (willen)

   _____

2 Erik: Ja, dat doe ik. (zullen)

   _____

3 Sanne: Breng je de stofzuiger even boven? (kunnen)

   _____

4 Erik: Drinken we eerst koffie? (zullen)

   _____

5 Sanne: Goed, zet jij dan even koffie? (willen)

   _____

6 Erik: Hè, ik doe hier altijd alles! (moeten)

   _____

Exercise 2.2

Conjugate the modal verbs.

   Situation: Erik and Sanne are in a restaurant.

1 Erik: (mogen)   _____ we bestellen?
2 Ober: (kunnen)   _____ u even wachten? Ik kom er zo aan.
3   (willen)   _____ u misschien iets drinken?
4 Erik: (mogen)   _____ ik even de wijnkaart zien?
5   (zullen)   Wat _____ we nemen, Sanne?
6 Sanne: (willen)   Ik _____ het liefst een droge rode wijn.
7 Ober: (kunnen)   Dan _____ u het beste de Malbec nemen.
8 Erik: (mogen)   En _____ ik dan een pilsje van u?
9 Ober: (zullen)   Natuurlijk. Ik _____ u ook de menukaart
                      brengen.
10 Erik: (willen)   Wat _____ jij eten, Sanne?

Exercise 2.3

Speaking exercise. From the list of activities below, select ones that you *can, must,* or *want* to do.

Example: Ik *moet* mijn huiswerk maken.

mijn kamer schoonmaken 'clean my room', naar de bioscoop gaan 'go to the movies', schaak spelen 'play chess', de tango dansen 'dance the tango', een kop koffie drinken 'drink coffee', een dutje doen 'take a nap', boodschappen doen 'get groceries', voor een test studeren 'study for a test', sporten 'exercise', de hond uitlaten 'walk the dog', televisie kijken 'watch TV', huiswerk maken 'do my homework', eten koken 'cook dinner', Frans spreken 'speak French', schaatsen 'skate', op vakantie gaan 'go on vacation'.

Write some of your sentences down.

_____

_____

_____

_____

UNIT THREE
Questions and question words

Introduction

In Dutch we distinguish between 'yes and no' questions and questions beginning with a question word. Both are characterized by the inversion of
subject and verb.

Examples for 'yes and no' questions

These questions begin with the conjugated verb, followed by the subject:

Heeft u vanavond tijd?   Do you have time tonight?
Ga je mee naar de bioscoop?   Are you going to the cinema with
me/us?
Is dit de trein naar Arnhem?   Is this the train to Arnhem?

Questions beginning with a question word
(or interrogative)

These questions begin with a question word, followed by the conjugated
verb, while the subject takes the third position in the sentence.

Hoe **heet je?**   What is your name?
Waar **woont u?**   Where do you live?
Wat **willen jullie vanavond eten?**   What would you like to eat
tonight?

Question words

hoe[1]	how	**welk/e**[3]	which
hoeveel[2]	how much/many	**wat voor**	what kind of
waar	where	**wie**[4]	who
waar ... vandaan	where from	**wanneer**[5]	when
wat	what	**waarom**	why

Notes

1 The word **hoe** can stand by itself 'how', as in **Hoe heet je?** 'What is your name?' or **Hoe vind je de film?** 'How do you like the movie?' or it can be combined with an adjective as in **Hoe oud ben je?** 'How old are you?' or **Hoe duur is de spinazie?** 'How much is the spinach?' or **Hoe groot is dat huis?** 'How big is that house?'.

2 **Hoeveel** can be followed by a noun in the singular (if this word is an uncountable noun that always appears in the singular, e.g. **koffie, thee, water**), as in **Hoeveel koffie drink je per dag?** 'How much coffee do you drink in a day?' or in the plural as in **Hoeveel kamers heeft dit huis?** 'How many rooms does this house have?'.

3 The word **welk** is for **het**-words such as **het huisnummer: Op welk huisnummer woon je?** 'What is your house number?'; **welke** is for **de**-words such as **de straat: In welke straat woon je?** 'What is your street name?', and for all nouns in the plural.

4 The pronunciation of **hoe** can be confusing: **wie** = who, and **hoe** = how!

5 The word **wanneer** is for 'when', but not when we talk about clock time. In that case we ask **hoe laat?** 'what time?'

Exercise 3.1

Which question words belong to which questions?

Situation: Karin is visiting her grandparents. Grandma asks a lot of questions.

1 Hoe   ___ eet je zo weinig?
2 Wie   ___ wil je eten?
3 Wanneer ___ gaat het op school?
4 Wat   ___ begint de zomervakantie?
5 Waarom ___ is je beste vriendin?

Exercise 3.2

Enter the correct question word.

Situation: Sanne's friends Henk and Marie Vanderveer just had a baby. Henk is at the town hall to register the birth of the baby. The desk person Ingrid is entering the data into the computer.

Ingrid	Henk
1 _____ is uw naam?	Henk Vanderveer.
2 _____ woont u?	Ik woon in Hardegarijp.
3 In _____ straat woont u?	In de Terpstraat.
4 En op _____ nummer?	Op nummer 45.
5 _____ is de baby geboren?	Op 4 mei.
6 _____ is ze geboren?	's Middags om kwart over drie.
7 _____ heet ze?	Isabel Annemarie.
8 _____ gaat het met de moeder?	Prima, dank u.

Exercise 3.3

Enter the correct question word.

Situation: Sanne is shopping for a new winter coat.

Verkoopster	Sanne
1 _____ kan ik voor u doen?	Ik zoek een winterjas.
2 _____ maat draagt u?	Ik heb maat 40.
3 _____ kleur zoekt u?	Hm, ik denk een rode of een zwarte.
4 _____ vindt u deze?	Leuk, _____ is de paskamer?
5 Daar, bij de blouses. _____ zit hij?	Prima. Ik neem deze.

Exercise 3.4

Enter the correct question word.

Situation: Sanne is shopping at the market.

Sanne	Groente- en kaasboer
1 _____ duur zijn de tomaten?	€2,50, mevrouw.
2 _____ appels zitten er in een pond?	Ongeveer vier.
3 _____ kost deze meloen?	€3,95.

17

4 _____ appels zijn zuurder,   De Elstar.
de Cox of de Elstar?

5 _____ komen deze   Uit Spanje.
sinasappels _____ ?

6 _____ zwaar is dat stuk kaas?   650 gram.

7 _____ kosten de eieren?   10 voor €3,95.

8 _____ krijgt u Meikaas binnen?   Volgende week, mevrouw.

9 _____ kaas is lekkerder, boeren-   Proeft u maar, mevrouw.
of komijn?

10 _____ vet zit er in die kaas?

60%, hmmm, lekker!

Exercise 3.5

What are the questions to the answers?

Situation: John is an American exchange student in the Netherlands. Shortly after his arrival, John goes to an orientation meeting at the university. He talks to some new friends.

Andere studenten   John
1 _____?   Ik heet John.
2 _____?   Smith.
3 _____?   Ik kom uit Wisconsin.
4 _____?   Ik studeer economie.
5 _____?   Een biertje, graag.

Exercise 3.6

Partner exercise. What are the questions to the answers?

Situation: John is looking for a place to live while he is studying in Utrecht. In the student paper, he reads an ad.:

Te huur:
Kamer in studentenhuis,
centrum Utrecht,
1 min. van buslijn 15.
Tel: 030-7562399

John calls the number, and asks many questions.

1 John: _____?
Verhuurder: De kamer is 26 vierkante meter.

2 John: _____?
Verhuurder: Nee, de kamer is niet gemeubileerd.

3 John: _____?
  Verhuurder: Ja, de kamer heeft een balkon.
4 John: _____?
  Verhuurder: U moet de keuken en de badkamer met drie personen delen.
5 John: _____?
  Verhuurder: Nee, u mag geen huisdieren hebben.
6 John: _____?
  Verhuurder: De huur is 350 euro per maand.
7 John: _____?
  Verhuurder: Kunt u dinsdagmiddag?
8 John: Ja, _____?
  Verhuurder: Om vier uur 's middags.
9 John: Goed. _____?
  Verhuurder: Rembrandtstraat 31.
10 John: O, _____?
  Verhuurder: Nee, u mag in de kamer niet roken.

Exercise 3.7

Put the questions in the correct word order and conjugate the underlined verbs.

Situation: John is at the train station. He asks about trains to Groningen and how to get to Groningen's city center once he gets there.

1 de trein – *vertrekken* – naar Groningen – Hoe laat
_____?

2 spoor – welk – de trein – Van – *vertrekken*
_____?

3 *kosten* – naar Groningen – een enkele reis – Wat
_____?

4 ik – hier – eten – *kunnen* – Waar – iets
_____?

5 van – ik – Hoe – het station in Groningen – *komen* – het centrum – naar
_____?

6 bus – *rijden* – Welke – het centrum – naar
_____?

7 ik – Hoeveel – nodig – strippen – *hebben*
_____?

8 de rit – Hoe lang – naar het centrum – *duren* – van het station
_____?

UNIT FOUR
Numbers and measures

Introduction

This chapter introduces you to cardinal and ordinal numbers. It includes sections on measures, currency units and dates.

Cardinal numbers

1	*één*	11	**elf**	10	**tien**	100	**honderd**
2	**twee**	12	**twaalf**	20	**twintig**	200	**tweehonderd**
3	**drie**	13	*dertien*	30	**dertig**	300	**driehonderd**
4	**vier**	14	*veertien*	40	**veertig**		. . .
5	**vijf**	15	**vijftien**	50	**vijftig**	1000	**duizend**
6	**zes**	16	**zestien**	60	**zestig**	10.000	**tienduizend**
7	**zeven**	17	**zeventien**	70	**zeventig**	100.000	**honderdduizend**
8	**acht**	18	**achttien**	80	*tachtig*	1.000.000	**één miljoen**
9	**negen**	19	**negentien**	90	**negentig**	1.000.000.000	**één miljard**
10	**tien**	20	**twintig**	100	*honderd*	0	**nul**

Counting up from 20, 30 and so on

In English, when we start counting up from 20, we think 'twenty plus one' ⇒ twenty-one. In Dutch we think 'one plus twenty', and so 21 = **eenentwintig**. Similarly, 31 = **eenendertig**. Counting up from 20 therefore goes as follows: **eenentwintig, tweeëntwintig, drieëntwintig, vierentwintig, vijfentwintig, zesentwintig, zevenentwintig, achtentwintig, negenentwintig, dertig.**

More examples

34	**vierendertig**	4398	**vierduizend driehonderdachtennegentig***
67	**zevenenzestig**	1314	**dertienhonderdveertien**
159	**honderdnegenenvijftig**	1003	**duizend drie**
375	**driehonderdvijfenzeventig**	2093	**tweeduizend drieënnegentig**

* Alternatively, 4398 could be pronounced **drieënveertighonderdachten- negentig**. This is possible in four digit numbers, but only when the second number is not a zero. There is no alternative form for **tweeduizend drieënnegentig**. Numbers are written as one word up to **duizend**. After **duizend**, they are separated. The numbers **miljoen**, **miljard**, and **biljoen** are separate words. More examples:

2220	**tweeduizend tweehonderdtwintig (tweeëntwintighonderdtwintig)**
2.220.222	**twee miljoen tweehonderdtwintigduizend tweehonderdtweeëntwintig**

Here's a nice tongue twister to practice your **ch** and **g**: **Achthonderdachtentachtig achtkantige kacheltjes** 'eight hundred and eighty-eight octangular little stoves'.

Spelling

The accents on **één** are intended to avoid confusion between the cardinal number 1 and the indefinite article **een**. Note the irregular spelling of 13 (**der**tien), 14 (**veer**tien) and 80 (**tachtig**). Also note the 'trema' on the unstressed **e** (at the start of a new syllable) in words such as **tweeëntwintig**, **drieënveertig**, etc.

Ordinal numbers

Ordinal numbers are used to indicate a certain order of things or events. The Dutch use two endings to form ordinal numbers: **-de** and **-ste**. See the examples in the table:

1–19 ⇒ **-de**

1e	*eerste*	11e	elfde
2e	tweede	12e	twaalfde
3e	*derde*	13e	dertiende
4e	vierde	14e	veertiende
5e	vijfde	15e	vijftiende
6e	zesde	16e	zestiende
7e	zevende	17e	zeventiende
8e	*achtste*	18e	achttiende
9e	negende	19e	negentiende
10e	tiende	105e	honderdvijfde

20 and up ⇒ **-ste**

20e	twintigste
21e	eenentwintigste
30e	dertigste
31e	eenendertigste
67e	zevenenzestigste
145e	honderdvijfenveertigste
380e	driehonderdtachtigste
1000e	duizendste
1.000.000e	miljoenste
1.000.000.000e	miljardste

Note the spelling of 1e (**eerste**), 3e (**derde**), which are not based on the cardinal number, and 8e (**achtste**) which ends in **-ste**. Following the rule that numbers are separated into more than one word after **duizend**, 2005e would be spelled **tweeduizend vijfde**.

Cardinal and ordinal numbers in dates

In English in the USA, we commonly write dates separated with forward slashes beginning with the month: 5/12/2007 (May 12, 2007). In Dutch, we separate the cardinal numbers of dates with dashes, and we begin with the day: 12-5-2007. The names of the months, not capitalized, are as follows: **januari, februari, maart, april, mei, juni, juli, augustus, september, oktober, november, december**. Examples:

1-1-1995	**één januari negentien(honderd)vijfennegentig**
6-8-1965	**zes augustus negentien(honderd)vijfenzestig**
3-3-2007	**drie maart tweeduizend zeven**

There are two main *prepositions* for dates: **op** for the day, and **in** for the year.

De baby is *op* 12 mei geboren.   The baby was born on May 12.
Harry studeert *in* 2008 af.   Harry will graduate in 2008.
De oorlog begon *op* 10 mei 1940.   The war started on May 10, 1940.

Ordinal numbers are often used in dates in Dutch, and they must be used if the month is not given. Examples:

Het is vandaag de zesentwintigste.   It is the twenty-sixth today.
Mijn verjaardag is de dertiende oktober.   My birthday is October 13th.

Cardinal numbers in currency units

The currency used in the Netherlands is the euro; its symbol is €. There are bills of 5, 10, 20, 50, 100, 200 and 500 euros. There are coins of 2 euros, 1 euro, 50 euro cents, 20 euro cents, 10 euro cents, 5 euro cents, 2 euro cents, and 1 euro cent.
Small amounts under 100 euros are written and pronounced as follows:

€3,75   **drie vijfenzeventig** (informal)
          drie euro vijfenzeventig (more formal)
          drie euro en vijfenzeventig cent (very formal)

Amounts above 100 euros are written and pronounced as follows:

€585,75   **vijfhonderdvijfentachtig vijfenzeventig** (informal)
          vijfhonderdvijfentachtig euro vijfenzeventig (more formal)
          vijfhonderdvijfentachtig euro en vijfenzeventig cent
          (very formal)

Note: The Dutch use commas in decimals instead of points. 7,5 is pronounced **zeven komma vijf**. The expression **nul komma nul** means 'ziltsch', 'nothing at all'.

Cardinal numbers in measures

The Dutch use the metric system, and therefore sizes and lengths are measured in meters, centimeters and millimeters (1 meter = 3.28 feet), and weight is measured in kilos, pounds and grams. There are plenty of online length and weight conversions available, so this is just a basic introduction to the most commonly used measures.

23

1 kilo (kg)	1000 gram (gr)	1 kilometer (km)	1000 meter
1 pond	500 gram	1 meter (m)	100 centimeter
1 ons	100 gram	1 centimeter (cm)	10 millimeter (mm)
1 liter (l)	10 deciliter (dl)	1 m²	1 vierkante meter

Examples

Erik koopt 3 kilo aardappelen.
Erik buys three kilos of apples.

De baby weegt 9 pond 32 gram.
The baby weighs 9 pounds and 32 grams.

De gemiddelde Nederlander gebruikt 124 liter water per dag.
The average Dutch person uses 124 liters of water every day.

Ik drink liters water per dag!
I drink liters of water each day.

Toen Sanne op dieet ging, vlogen de ponden eraf.
When Sanne went on a diet, she lost pound after pound.

Erik gaat elke dag 30 kilometer fietsen.
Erik bikes 30 kilometers every day.

Peter is nu 1,86 m (pronounced **één meter zesentachtig**) **lang.**
Peter is 1.86 m tall now.

We moeten nog kilometers lopen naar de volgende stranttent.
We still have to walk miles and miles to the next beach restaurant.

Mijn woonkamer is 25 m² (vierkante meter).
My living room is 25 square meters.

Note: Measure units are used in the **singular** after a cardinal number or the words **hoeveel** 'how much', 'how many', **zoveel** 'that much/many' and **een paar** 'a few', 'a couple'. However, when a measure unit is used with emphasis or as an object in itself, it appears in the plural. Note the differences in the examples:

1 **Het broodje kaas kostte drie euro.**
   The cheese sandwich cost three euros.

2 **Hij had drie euro's in z'n zak.**
   He had three euros in his pocket.

In sentence 1, a specific *amount* is meant; in sentence 2, the three euro *coins* are meant.

3 **Ik heb twee meter stof voor de jurk gekocht.**
I bought two meters of material for the dress.

4 **Gisteren heb ik in de uitverkoop meters stof gekocht!**
Yesterday, in the sale, I bought meters and meters of material.

In sentence 3, we are talking about a specific amount; in sentence 4, the
measure unit is used with a lot of emphasis.

5 **Ina is tijdens haar vakantie 2 kilo aangekomen.**
Ina gained 2 kilos during her vacation.

6 **Ina is tijdens haar vakantie kilo's aangekomen!**
Ina gained (many) kilos during her vacation!

Again, in sentence 5, the speaker talks about an exact amount; in sentence
6, the speaker wants to stress that Ina gained pounds and pounds.
$1/2$ = **(een) half**, $1^1/_2$ = **anderhalf** (**één en een half**). These fractions are
used mostly as adjectives, and so they follow the rules for adjective endings. Therefore: **een half brood** (**het**-word), **een halve appel**, **anderhalve
kilo kaas**, **de helft** = 'the half' ⇒ **Ik eet de helft van de pizza**. 'I eat half
of the pizza'.

Indefinite numbers

veel many, much	**verschillende** various	**enig(e)** some	**genoeg** enough
weinig little, few	**verscheidene** various	**menig(e)** many	**voldoende** enough
enkele a few	**sommige** some	**een paar** a few	**wat** some, a little

Indefinite numbers are used when we refer to an unspecified number of
things. Examples:

Sanne kocht verscheidene broodjes. Sanne bought various rolls.
Is er nog genoeg kaas in huis? Is there enough cheese in the house?

Note that **een paar** can mean 'a few' or 'a pair'. Examples:

Peter eet een paar dropjes. Peter eats a few licorice drops.
Ik heb een paar nieuwe schoenen gekocht. I bought a pair of new shoes.

25

Note also the difference between **sommige** and **soms**, often confused by English learners of Dutch. The word **sommige** means 'some', and **soms** means 'sometimes'.

An **-n** added to indefinite numbers such as **vele**, **sommige**, and **enkele** indicates that they refer to people only. Examples:

Velen kwamen naar het feest.
Many people came to the party.

Sommigen bleven tot middernacht op het feest.
Some stayed at the party til midnight.

Ik heb enkelen van u al ontmoet.
I have already met some of you.

beide, beiden, allebei

The definite number **beide** 'both' can be used as an adjective or independently. When used as an adjective, it can refer to persons and things, and when used independently, it refers to things only. Examples:

Beide studenten zijn voor het examen gezakt.
Both students failed the exam.

Beide bomen overleefden de droogte.
Both trees survived the drought.

De brieven zijn beide voor mij.
Both letters are for me.

The definite number **beiden** refers only to people, and it is used independently.

Erik en Sanne komen beiden naar het feest.
Both Erik and Sanne will come to the party.

The definite number **allebei** refers to people and things. It follows the noun to which it refers. Examples:

Ik heb die twee truien allebei gekocht.
I bought both those sweaters.

Erik en Sanne komen allebei naar het feest.
Both Erik and Sanne will come to the party.

26   The expression **geen van beide/beiden** 'neither' follows the rules above.

Erik en Sanne komen geen van beiden naar het feest.
Neither Erik nor Sanne is coming to the party.

Ik heb een trui en een broek gepast, maar ik heb ze geen van beide gekocht.
I tried a sweater and a pair of pants, but I bought neither.

Exercise 4.1

Say the numbers.

a	3	d	35	g	1007	j	1962
b	11	e	267	h	1580	k	4020
c	14	f	894	i	2356	l	45.627

Exercise 4.2

Write out the dates as you would say them.

1 21-5-1983 _____
2 3-12-2006 _____
3 9-9-1999   _____
4 6-1-1975   _____
5 12-3-2002 _____

Exercise 4.3

Write out the date using an ordinal number.

Example: 5 mei ⇒ de vijfde mei.

1 12 september ⇒ _____
2 9 oktober ⇒ _____
3 30 april ⇒ _____
4 14 juni ⇒ _____
5 26 december ⇒ _____

Exercise 4.4

Answer the questions following the example, and *write out the numbers and measures* as you would say them in the answers. The last two are *ordinal numbers*.

Example: Lisa, hoe lang ben jij? (1,73 m) ⇒ Ik ben één meter drieënzeventig.

1   Nico, hoeveel biertjes drink je per dag? (3) Ik drink _____ biertjes per dag.
2   Berend, hoe groot is je kamer? (16 m²) Mijn kamer is _____
3   Selma, wanneer ben je jarig? (15 juli) Ik ben op _____ _____ jarig.
4   Sjoerd, hoe lang ben jij? (1,92 m) Ik ben _____
5   Achmed, hoe zwaar ben jij? (82 kg) Ik weeg _____
6   Jeanne, hoe ver fiets je naar school? (13 km) Ik fiets _____ _____
7   Michael, heb je geld bij je? (€10,80) Ja, ik heb _____ _____ bij me.
8   Patrick, wat kostte jouw fiets? (€489) Mijn fiets kostte _____ _____
9   Sven, drink je niet te veel koffie? (8) Ja, dit is mijn _____ _____ kopje!
10   Remco, in welke klas zit je? (5) Ik zit in de _____

Exercise 4.5

Sanne's shopping list. Write the numbers and measurements as you would say them.

1   (5 kg) _____ aardappelen
2   (1½ pond) _____ oude kaas
3   (2 l) _____ melk
4   (100 gr) _____ champignons
5   (½) _____ bruin brood

Exercise 4.6

Which one is correct? The singular or the plural form? Underline it.

1 Sanne koopt elke week drie kilo/kilo's aardappelen op de markt.
2 Ze fietst twee kilometers/kilometer naar de markt.
3 Haar kinderen drinken liter/liters melk per week.
4 En hoeveel pond/ponden kaas eten ze per week?
5 O, ik denk wel een paar kilo's/kilo.

Exercise 4.7

Write the word between brackets in the correct form. Sometimes it is a cardinal number, sometimes it is an ordinal number.

Situation: Erik shows family pictures.

1 (één)   Kijk, dit was ons _____ huis. Wat was dat klein!
2 (twee)   Dit is Karin, ons _____ kind, als baby.
3 (twintig) Ze is op _____ januari jarig. Dit was in de winter van 1985.
4 (drie)   Dit is Peter in zijn _____ weekendjob, als kelner in een café.
5 (vier)   Dit is Sanne met _____ vriendinnen in Parijs.
6 (veertig) Dit was de _____ trouwdag van mijn ouders.
7 (honderd) Er waren wel _____ mensen op dat feest.
8 (vijftig) Dit was de _____ verjaardag van Sanne's zus Linda.
9 (tien)   Dit was in Engeland. Daar zijn we wel _____ keer geweest.
10 (acht)   Dit is de oude Peugeot, dat was mijn _____ auto.

UNIT FIVE
Telling the time

Introduction

This unit discusses many aspects of time, with an emphasis on adverbs and prepositions.

Starting with some examples

Gisteren gingen we naar de film. De film begon *om acht uur. Daarna* dronken we een biertje. *Zaterdagavond* gaan we naar een concert. En *volgende week* naar Amsterdam!

Yesterday, we went to a movie. It started at eight. Afterwards, we had a beer. Saturday evening, we will go to a concert. And next week, to Amsterdam!

The week

eergisteren	the day before yesterday
gisteren	yesterday
vandaag	today
morgen	tomorrow
overmorgen	the day after tomorrow
maandag	Monday
dinsdag	Tuesday
woensdag	Wednesday
donderdag	Thursday
vrijdag	Friday
zaterdag	Saturday
zondag	Sunday

The day

6–12	**de morgen/ochtend** morning	18–24	**de avond** evening	
12–18	**de middag** afternoon	24–6	**de nacht** night	

vanmorgen	this morning
vanmiddag	this afternoon
vanavond	this evening
vannacht	tonight
's morgens	every morning, in the morning
's middags	every afternoon, in the afternoon
's avonds	every evening, in the evening
's nachts	every night, at night

Combining it all

morgenochtend	tomorrow morning
gister(en)middag	yesterday afternoon
woensdagmiddag	Wednesday afternoon
dinsdagavond	Tuesday evening

The days of the week are not capitalized, unless they are the first word of the sentence. The parts of the week, the parts of the day, and the names of the week days can be combined to form more specific expressions of time such as **zaterdagavond**, **zondagmorgen**, **gistermiddag**, etc. In combinations with **gisteren**, the **-en** is optional.

We use the *apostrophe s plus s* at the end of the time expression (an old genitive case) to indicate that something is happening *regularly*. **'s maandags** (old: **des maandags**) is therefore 'every Monday'. **'s morgens** means 'every morning'. We also use the *apostrophe s plus s* for two of the seasons: **'s winters** 'in winter', **'s zomers** 'in summer'. But: **in de lente** 'in spring', **in de herfst** 'in fall'.

Note: The **'s** in expressions such as **'s zondags**, **'s maandags** is sometimes dropped. It is a matter of preference in which pronunciation is an important factor. It is easier, for example, to pronounce **donderdags** than **'s donderdags**. Also, do not confuse **avond** with **nacht**. Everything before midnight is **avond**. 'Let's go to the bar Saturday night' is in Dutch: **Laten we** *zaterdagavond* **naar de bar gaan**. Then, if it was a long night, you could say in Dutch: **Ik ben** *zaterdagnacht* **om drie uur thuisgekomen**. 'Saturday night I came home at three in the morning.'

Adjectives and adverbs

Expressions of time can be used to form adjectives and adverbs. Examples:

de tijd – tijdelijk	temporary/-ily
de dag – dagelijks	daily
de week – wekelijks	weekly
de maand – maandelijks	monthly
het jaar – jaarlijks	yearly
maandag – maandags	of/on Monday

Examples

een tijdelijk baantje 'a temporary job', **een dagelijkse krant** 'a daily paper', **een wekelijkse column** 'a weekly column', **een maandelijkse vergadering** 'a monthly meeting', **een jaarlijks onderzoek** 'a yearly exam', **de maandagse yogales** 'the yoga class on Monday'.

Clock time

	How we say it	Alternative
12:00	**Het is twaalf uur.**	
12:05	**Het is vijf over twaalf.**	**Het is twaalf uur vijf.**
12:10	**Het is tien over twaalf.**	**Het is twaalf uur tien.**
12:15	**Het is kwart over twaalf.**	**Het is twaalf uur vijftien.**
12:20	**Het is twintig over twaalf/tien voor half één.**	**Het is twaalf uur twintig.**
12:25	**Het is vijf voor half één.**	**Het is twaalf uur vijfentwintig.**
12:30	**Het is half één.**	**Het is twaalf uur dertig.**
12:35	**Het is vijf over half één.**	**Het is twaalf uur vijfendertig.**
12:40	**Het is twintig voor één/tien over half één.**	**Het is twaalf uur veertig.**
12:45	**Het is kwart voor één.**	**Het is twaalf uur vijfenveertig.**
12:50	**Het is tien voor één.**	**Het is twaalf uur vijftig.**
12:55	**Het is vijf voor één.**	**Het is twaalf uur vijfenvijftig.**
13:00	**Het is één uur.**	**Het is dertien uur.**
1:00	**Het is één uur 's nachts.**	

Examples in context

Hoe laat **is het? Het is kwart over vijf.**
What time is it? It is a quarter past five.

Hoe laat **begint de les? Om twee uur.**
What time does the class start? At two o'clock.

Hoe laat **ga je meestal naar bed? Ik ga meestal om half twaalf naar bed.**
What time do you usually go to bed? I usually go to bed at eleven thirty.

Hoe laat **kom je vanavond? Ik kom vanavond tegen acht uur.**
What time will you come tonight? I will come around eight tonight.

Note: The word **uur** in clock time is only used on the full hour: **acht uur**, **twaalf uur** and so on. In all other cases we do not say **uur**: **half twaalf**, **kwart over drie**, **tien over half zeven** and so on.

Time in the plural: dag, maand, week, eeuw, minuut, seconde

Het heeft drie *dagen* **geregend.**
It rained for three days.

De schoolvakantie duurt twee *maanden.*
The school vacation lasts two months.

Over twee *weken* **ga ik op vakantie.**
I go on vacation in two weeks.

Dit geneesmiddel werkt al *eeuwen***!**
This medication has worked for centuries.

Hoeveel *minuten* **kun je hardlopen?**
How many minutes can you run for?

De aardbeving duurde vijftien *seconden.*
The earthquake lasted fifteen seconds.

Time in the singular: uur, kwartier, jaar, keer (= maal)

Hennie studeert drie *uur* **per dag.**
Hennie studies three hours a day.

We wachten al drie *kwartier***!**
We've been waiting for three quarters of an hour.

Het kind van Nico en Lisa is tien *jaar* oud.
Nico and Lisa's child is ten years old.

Erik speelt twee *keer* per week tennis.
Erik plays tennis two times (twice) a week.

Sanne sport twee *maal* (tweemaal) per week.
Sanne exercises twice a week.

After a cardinal number, the words **uur**, **kwartier**, **jaar**, **keer** and **maal** appear in the singular. They can also appear in the plural, in expressions such as **De jaren gaan snel voorbij** 'The years go by fast', **We zaten uren te kletsen!** 'We chatted for hours!'.

Prepositions in time expressions

geleden ago	**na** after	**om** at, **op** on	**over** in
rond around	**tegen** just before	**tijdens** during	**tot** until
tussen between	**van–tot** from–til	**vanaf** beginning at	**voor** before

Peter studeert een uur *voor* de les. *Na* de les drinkt hij een kopje koffie. *Tijdens* de les maakt hij notities. *Tussen* de lessen praat hij met vrienden. *Om* vijf uur gaat hij naar huis. *Rond* zes uur eet hij avondeten. *Tegen* acht uur zet hij de televisie aan. *Over* een paar minuten begint het journaal. Het journaal duurt *tot* twintig over acht. Peter kijkt *van* acht *tot* negen televisie. Karin is een uur *geleden* thuisgekomen. *Vanaf* gisteren heeft ze elke dinsdag volleybaltraining.
Peter studies for an hour *before* class. *After* class, he drinks a cup of coffee. *During* class, he takes notes. *Between* classes, he talks to friends. He goes home *at* five. He eats dinner *around* six. He turns the TV on *just before* eight. The news will begin *in* a few minutes. The news lasts *until* twenty past eight. Peter watches TV *from* eight *until* nine. Karin came home an hour *ago*. *Beginning* yesterday, she has volleyball training every Tuesday.

Note that **geleden** is a so-called *post*position; it follows the noun (see also Unit 25).

Some verbs: beginnen, eindigen, duren

De les *begint* om drie uur.	The class starts at three.
De les *eindigt* om half vijf.	The class ends at four thirty.
De les *duurt* dus anderhalf uur.	The class lasts an hour and a half.

Adverbs: altijd – meestal – vaak – regelmatig – soms – zelden – nooit

Adverbs: altijd – meestal – vaak – regel- matig – soms – zelden – nooit

De eetgewoonten van Erik en zijn familie (Erik and his family's eating habits)

We drinken *altijd* water bij het eten. *Meestal* eten we aardappels, vlees en groente. We eten ook *vaak* pasta of rijst. Ik maak *regelmatig* een flesje wijn open. *Soms* gaan we naar de pizzeria. We halen *zelden* iets van de Chinees. We eten *nooit* bij McDonald's.
We *always* drink water with our dinner. *Most of the time (usually)* we eat potatoes, meat, and vegetables. We also *often* eat pasta or rice. I *regularly* open a bottle of wine. *Sometimes* we go to the pizzeria. We *seldom* go to the Chinese take-out. We *never* eat at McDonald's.

Note: Adverbs of time usually follow the conjugated verb, unless the adverb begins the sentence. When the sentence begins with the adverb, the verb stays in the second place, and the subject moves to the third place (inversion of subject and verb).

Order of events: eerst, dan (toen), daarna, vervolgens, verder, tenslotte

Wat doet Erik meestal op zaterdag? What does Erik typically do on Saturday?

Eerst drinkt hij koffie en leest hij de krant van a tot z. *Dan* gaat hij een rondje hardlopen. *Daarna* gaat hij met Sanne naar de markt. *Vervolgens* wast hij de auto. *Verder* doet hij nog wat klussen rond het huis en *tenslotte* kijkt hij met de familie televisie.
First, he drinks coffee and he reads the paper cover to cover. *Then* he goes jogging for a bit. *Afterwards*, he goes to the market with Sanne. *Next*, he washes the car. *Then (or next)*, he does some chores around the house and *lastly*, he watches TV with the family.

Note: If this story had been told in the *past tense*, you would have had to use **toen** instead of **dan**. *Toen is always used in the past tense.*

Adverbs: net, pas, al, nu, toen, straks, vroeg(er), laat, ooit, binnenkort

Ik ben *net* wakker.	I *just* woke up.
De winkel is *pas* geopend.	The store *recently* opened.
De bus komt *pas* over een uur.	The bus will *not* come *for* another hour.
De bus is er *al*.	The bus is *already* here.
Moeten we dit *nu* doen?	Do we have to do this *now*?
***Toen* ging ik naar huis.**	*Then* I went home.
Tot *straks*.	See you *later*.
Erik staat altijd *vroeg* op.	Erik always gets up *early*.
De bus is vandaag te *laat*.	The bus is *late* today.
***Vroeger* kon je in dit meer zwemmen.**	You *used to* be able to swim in this lake.
***Ooit* wil ik weer eens naar Engeland.**	*Some day* I want to go to England again.
***Binnenkort* ga ik verhuizen.**	I will *soon* move.

Note: Most of these adverbs speak for themselves and have equivalents in English. Some are more difficult to translate literally into English, such as **pas**. As you notice in the examples, this word can have different meanings depending on the context (either 'recently' or 'not until', 'not for'). A word about **straks**: It means 'later, but on the same day'. Saying **tot straks** 'see you later' means you will see the other person again the same day. Otherwise you'd have to say **tot morgen** 'see you tomorrow', **tot volgende week** 'see you next week', **tot de volgende keer** 'see you next time', etc.

Odds and ends

1 Dutch uses **vorig** for 'last', and **volgend** for 'next'. These words follow the rules for adjective endings. Examples: **vorig jaar** 'last year', **vorige week** 'last week', **volgend jaar** 'next year', **volgende week** 'next week'.
2 When something happens every day or week, we say **elke dag, elke week**; when it happens with intermissions, we say, for example, **om de andere dag** 'every other day', **om de drie weken** 'every third week'.
3 Talking about centuries, we use ordinal numbers: **de twintigste eeuw** 'the twentieth century', **de negentiende eeuw** 'the nineteenth century'.
4 Talking about decades, there are a few options: **de zeventiger jaren** 'the seventies', **de jaren vijftig** 'the fifties'.

Exercise 5.1

What time is it on these clocks?

1 _____   2 _____   3 _____

4 _____   5 _____

Exercise 5.2

Look at the pictures and answer the questions in full sentences.

1 Hoe laat wordt Erik 's morgens wakker? _____
2 Hoe laat zit Erik in een vergadering? _____

Exercise 5.3

Look at Sanne's schedule, then answer the questions following the examples: 37

Examples: Wanneer gaat Sanne naar de film? *Sanne gaat maandagavond*
naar de film.
Hoe laat is de yogales? *De yogales is om vier uur.*

maandag	*dinsdag*	*woensdag*
8:00–12:00 werken	8:00–12:00 werken	8:00–12:00 werken
16:00 yoga	14.15 dokter Meijer	12:00 lunch met Hennie
20:00 film met Linda	19:30 schoolvergadering	15:45 computerles

donderdag	*vrijdag*	*zaterdag*
8:00–12:00 werken	10.00 koffie met Sara	20.00 Mieke en Hans
15.10 Karin tandarts	16.00 Amnesty-groep	
19:00 tennis		*zondag*

1 Wanneer speelt Sanne tennis?   _____
2 Wanneer komen Mieke en Hans?   _____
3 Wanneer gaat Sanne naar de Amnesty-groep?   _____
4 Wanneer werkt Sanne niet?   _____
5 Wanneer drinkt ze koffie met Sara?   _____

6 Hoe laat gaat Sanne naar de film?   _____
7 Hoe laat moet ze naar dokter Meijer?   _____
8 Hoe laat moet Karin naar de tandarts?   _____
9 Hoe laat is de computerles?   _____
10 Hoe laat is de schoolvergadering?   _____

Exercise 5.4

Use the correct adverb: **al**, **net**, **pas**, **straks**, **vroeg**, **laat**, **nu**, **toen**, **ooit**,
binnenkort.

Persoon A	Persoon B
O nee! Daar gaat de bus.	Ja, we zijn te _____ (1).
Kom vanmiddag even koffie drinken.	Goed, tot _____ (2).
Ik ga _____ (3) op vakantie.	Wat leuk! Waarnaartoe?
Ben jij weleens geopereerd?	Ja, ik was _____ (4) zes jaar oud.
Is het _____ (5) tien voor acht?	Ja, we moeten ons haasten.
Ik ga even tennissen.	_____ (6)?? We eten over vijf minuten!
Tanja gaat op een cruise naar Aruba.	Leuk, dat wil ik _____ (7) ook eens doen.
Kom, we gaan in de tuin werken.	Rustig zeg, ik ben _____ (8) wakker!

Ik sta meestal om half zes op. Jemig, dat is _____ (9)!
Schiet op, de bus komt over 5 minuten. Nee, de bus komt _____ (10) over 20 minuten.

Exercise 5.5

Speaking exercise. Look at the list of activities below and tell your partner what you do **altijd**, **meestal**, **vaak**, **regelmatig**, **soms**, **zelden**, **nooit**.

Example: Ik doe *regelmatig* sport.

Activiteiten: ontbijt eten, email schrijven, studeren, televisie kijken, sport doen, het huis schoonmaken, met mijn moeder telefoneren, met vrienden telefoneren, naar de kerk gaan, boodschappen doen, de auto wassen, naar school fietsen, in een restaurant eten, op reis gaan, mijn familie bezoeken, met de hond wandelen, de krant lezen.

UNIT SIX
Articles and nouns

Introduction

This chapter discusses definite and indefinite articles and nouns. It also offers a brief introduction to compound nouns.

Articles

In Dutch we have the definite articles **de** and **het** 'the' and the indefinite article **een** 'a'. The article **de** is for masculine and feminine (or common) nouns, and the article **het** is for neuter nouns. Examples are **de auto** 'the car', **het huis** 'the house', **een straat** 'a street'. It is impossible to give rules for why nouns are common or neuter, however, the number of **de**-words is about twice as large as the number of **het**-words. For learning purposes, it is best to memorize words *with* their articles.

Countable or uncountable?

All nouns, countable or uncountable, can appear with a definite article. In the plural, all nouns have the definite article **de**. The indefinite article **een**, however, can only appear with countable nouns in the singular. If the noun is uncountable (for example **suiker**, **water**, **koffie**, **thee**), it appears without an article. Indefinite countable nouns in the plural do not have an article. For clarification, here is an overview:

| | Definite | | Indefinite | | Examples in context |
	Countable	Uncountable	Countable	Uncountable	
Singular	de straat	het ijs	een straat	ijs	
Plural	de straten	-	- straten	-	
Singular	het huis	de koffie	een huis	koffie	
Plural	de huizen	-	- huizen	-	

Examples in context

1 **Erik bestelt koffie.** *De* **koffie is lekker.**
Erik orders coffee. The coffee tastes good.

2 **Ik heb** *een* **klein huis.** *Het* **huis van mijn buurman is veel groter.**
I have a small house. My neighbor's house is much bigger.

3 *De* **straten zijn nat van de regen.**
The streets are wet from the rain.

4 **Er ligt ijs op het water.** *Het* **ijs is dun.**
There is ice on the water. The ice is thin.

An indefinite noun such as **koffie** in example 1 and **een huis** in example 2 is used to either first introduce a subject or object about which the listener doesn't know anything yet, or to make a very general statement about it. A definite noun such as **de koffie** in example 1 and **het huis** in example 2 is used when the listener already knows the subject or object or when the speaker gives it particular qualities or characteristics. The translations demonstrate that it works the exact same way in English.

The indefinite article with an affiliation

In English, when one talks about what a person does for work, we say, for example, 'Peter is a teacher'. In Dutch, however, we do not use the indefinite article in this case. Instead we say: **'Peter is leraar'** or **'Peter is leraar van beroep'**. The same happens when we talk about our affiliation with a country, a city, a religion: **'Peter is Nederlander'**, **'Peter is Amsterdammer'**, **'Peter is christen'**. However, when an adjective or any other qualifying notion is added, these affiliations will appear with the indefinite article **een**.

Peter is *een* **uitstekende leraar.**
Peter is an outstanding teacher.

Peter is *een* leraar met veel ervaring.
Peter is a teacher with much experience.

Peter is *een* 24-jarige Nederlander.
Peter is a 24-year-old Dutchman.

Peter is *een* echte Amsterdammer.
Peter is a real Amsterdammer.

Also, when talking about affiliations in a general sense, we use the indefinite article. In the plural, of course, we do not have an article.

Een leraar heeft veel werk te doen.
A teacher has a lot of work to do.

Leraren verdienen best veel.
Teachers make quite a bit of money.

Compound nouns

Two words can be used to make one new word, for example **de bank +
de rekening = de bankrekening** 'bank account', **de post + het kantoor =
het postkantoor** 'post office'. In English, many compound words are separated (see *bank account*), but in Dutch they are written together as one
word. Note that the gender of the compound noun is determined by the
gender of the *second* word: ***de* wijn + *het* glas = *het* wijnglas**. For more
information on word formation and derivation, check *Intermediate Dutch:
A Grammar and Workbook*.

Exercise 6.1

Are the underlined nouns definite or indefinite?

1 <u>Het gezin</u> van Erik woont in Hardegarijp. _____
2 Hij heeft <u>een huis</u> in de schildersbuurt. _____
3 Erik werkt voor <u>een verzekeringsbank</u>. _____
4 Erik gaat met <u>de bus</u> naar zijn werk. _____
5 Bij de lunch drinkt Erik <u>koffie</u>. _____

Exercise 6.2

Enter **de**, **het**, **een** or nothing (–).

Situation: Sanne and Monique are in a café.

Sanne en Monique zijn in _____ (1) café. _____ (2) ober neemt _____
(3) bestelling op. Sanne bestelt _____ (4) thee. "Met _____ (5) melk en
_____ (6) suiker?," vraagt _____ (7) ober. "Nee, geeft u mij maar _____
(8) beetje citroen," zegt Sanne. Monique heeft liever _____ (9) kopje koffie.
En ze heeft _____ (10) honger, dus ze bestelt ook _____ (11) broodje kaas.
Sanne neemt _____ (12) stuk warme appeltaart. Na tien minuten komt _____
(13) ober en vraagt: "Hoe smaakt _____ (14) broodje kaas?" Monique
antwoordt: "_____ (15) kaas op _____ (16) broodje is te zout." "En hoe
is _____ (17) appeltaart?," vraagt hij. "_____ (18) appeltaart is droog," zegt
Sanne. "Ach, wat jammer," zegt hij. Tegen _____ (19) collega zegt hij: "Ik
heb vandaag _____ (20) slechte dag."

Exercise 6.3

Make compound words with words from the left column and from the right
column. Include the article.

Situation: The cashier is ringing up Erik's items in the supermarket.

het toilet	de vla	1 _____	toilet . . .
de pinda	de melk	2 _____	pinda . . .
de koffie	het papier	3 _____	koffie . . .
de boter	de crème	4 _____	boter . . .
de was	het water	5 _____	was . . .
het poeder	de salade	6 _____	poeder . . .
de tand	de kaas	7 _____	tand . . .
de chocolade	het middel	8 _____	chocolade . . .
de soep	de koek	9 _____	soep . . .
de aardappel	het vlees	10 _____	aardappel . . .
de hand	de suiker	11 _____	hand . . .
de bron	de pasta	12 _____	bron . . .

Exercise 6.4

Enter **de**, **het**, **een**, or nothing (–).

*Situation: A fashion show of commuters. You will meet three people on
the bus to work. They will be introduced to you by what they do for their
job and what they wear.*

43

A Erik: Hallo, mijn naam is Erik. Ik ben _____ (1) advocaat. Ik werk in _____ (2) bank. Voor mijn werk draag ik meestal _____ (3) nette kleren. Vandaag draag ik _____ (4) broek en _____ (5) jasje. _____ (6) jasje is donkerblauw, _____ (7) broek is grijs. Als we met _____ (8) klanten werken, moeten we _____ (9) stropdas dragen. Maar thuis draag ik nooit _____ (10) stropdas!

B Tina: Hoi, ik ben Tina, ik ben _____ (1) studente. Ik ben op weg naar _____ (2) universiteit. Op college draag ik meestal _____ (3) lekker makkelijke kleren, _____ (4) spijkerbroek of zo met _____ (5) t-shirt of _____ (6) trui. Maar vandaag moet ik naar _____ (7) interview voor _____ (8) job. Daarom draag ik _____ (9) rok en _____ (10) bloes.

C Bas: Dag, ik ben Bas en ik werk bij _____ (1) politie. Ik moet dus _____ (2) uniform dragen. _____ (3) uniform is blauw, en ik draag _____ (4) zwarte schoenen. _____ (5) schoenen moeten comfortabel zitten, want ik loop veel door _____ (6) stad. Soms werk ik op _____ (7) bureau in Amsterdam-Zuid. Dan draag ik _____ (8) jasje en _____ (9) pet niet. Maar _____ (10) lichtblauwe overhemd moet ik dan toch wel aanhebben.

UNIT SEVEN
The plural of nouns

Introduction

While the rules for the formation of the plural of nouns are simple, as there are only two endings, we need to pay special attention to spelling. Some of the rules discussed in Unit 1 on verb conjugation apply to the formation of the plural of nouns as well. As mentioned in Unit 6, the definite article for the plural is always **de**.

The formation of the plural: -en or -s

The ending **-s**

This is used in the following cases:

1 Words ending in unstressed **-er**, **-el**, **-em**, **-en**, **-erd**, and sometimes **-aar**.

de kamer	room	**de kamers**
de lepel	spoon	**de lepels**
de bezem	broom	**de bezems**
de deken	blanket	**de dekens**
de buizerd	buzzard	**de buizerds**
de metselaar	mason	**de metselaars**

2 Words ending in the vowels **a, o, u, i, y**. An apostrophe is added. Also words ending in unstressed **-e** and **-ie**, no apostrophe is added. Lastly, loanwords ending in **-é**, again without the apostrophe, and other loanwords (**film, telefoon, restaurant**).

de agenda	calendar	**de agenda's**
de auto	car	**de auto's**
de baby	baby	**de baby's**
de vakantie	vacation	**de vakanties**
de paraplu	umbrella	**de paraplu's**

de taxi	taxi	de taxi's
de garage	garage	de garages
het café	café	de cafés

3 All diminutives ending in **-je** (and **-tje**, **-pje**, **-kje**).

het tasje	small bag	de tasjes
het deurtje	small door	de deurtjes
het armpje	small arm	de armpjes
het vinkje	small finch	de vinkjes

4 Words for persons ending in **-e**, **-ster**, **-ier**, **-eur** and **-or**.

de dame	lady	de dames
de werkster	cleaner	de werksters
de amateur	amateur	de amateurs
de koetsier	coach driver	de koetsiers

Of course, there are no rules without exceptions. Sometimes you might find two plural forms for a word, such as **aardappels** and **aardappelen** 'potatoes', **wortels** and **wortelen** 'carrots' or **gedachtes** and **gedachten** 'thoughts'. In words for persons ending in **-eur** and **-or**, we often find two plural forms, for example in **directeur–directeurs/directeuren** 'directors', or in **professor–professors/professoren** 'professors'. Other plural forms will contradict the rule, such as **redenen** instead of **redens** 'reasons' or **wonderen** instead of **wonders** 'miracles'.

The ending -en

This is used in all other cases. The number of words that form the plural with the ending **-en** is much larger than the number of plural forms ending in **-s** or 'apostrophe-**s**'.

de kaart	map, ticket	de kaarten
het boek	book	de boeken
de kerk	church	de kerken
het woord	word	de woorden

The *spelling rules* are similar to those applied in verb conjugation. For instance, if the word in the singular has a long, double vowel followed by a single consonant in a closed syllable, the syllable opens when the ending **-en** is added, and one vowel is dropped.

de maan	moon	de manen
de boom	tree	de bomen
het been	leg	de benen
het uur	hour	de uren

When the plural ending **-en** is added to a syllable with a short vowel followed by a single consonant, that consonant is doubled. This happens in many one-syllable words, but also in longer or compound words ending in a closed syllable with a short vowel.

de kip	chicken	de kippen
de ton	barrel	de tonnen
de asbak	ashtray	de asbakken
de bril	glasses	de brillen

Some words ending in **-ie** have the plural ending **-en** or **-n**. If **-ie** is stressed, the ending **-en** results in a double **-e**. To separate the ending **-en** in the pronunciation of the plural form, we put a 'trema' (diaeresis) on the second **-e**. Examples:

de melodie	melody	de melodieën
de knie	knee	de knieën

If **-ie** is unstressed, we add the ending **-n** and put a 'trema' on **-e**. Examples:

de bacterie	germ	de bacteriën
de porie	pore	de poriën

Lastly, the letters **-f** or **-s** preceded by a long vowel or a diphthong become voiced when the ending **-en** is added, so **-s** turns into **-z**, and **-f** into **-v**.

het huis	house	de huizen
de vaas	vase	de vazen
de hoef	hoof	de hoeven
de zeef	strainer	de zeven

The same change occurs in words ending in **-lf**, **-rf**, **-ms**, **-ns**, **-rs** preceded by a short or long vowel or diphthong.

de wolf	wolf	de wolven
de scherf	fragment	de scherven
de gems	chamois	de gemzen

de gans	goose	**de ganzen**
de laars	boot	**de laarzen**
de beurs	wallet	**de beurzen**

Exceptions are words ending in **-aaf**: **fotograaf–fotografen** 'photographer' or **-oof**: **filosoof–filosofen** 'philosopher'; also **elf–elfen** 'elf', **kruis–kruisen** 'cross', **eis–eisen** 'demand', **dans–dansen** 'dance', **mens–mensen** 'person', **kous–kousen** 'stocking'.

Irregular plural forms

There are many irregular plural forms. Some words with a short vowel **-a-**, **-e-** or **-o-** followed by a single consonant do not double the consonant in the plural:

het dak	roof	**de daken**
het glas	glass	**de glazen**
de weg	road, way	**de wegen**
het slot	lock	**de sloten**

Some words change the vowel in the plural, $a \Rightarrow e$, $i \Rightarrow e$:

de stad	city	**de steden**
het schip	ship	**de schepen**

Some words form the plural with the ending **-eren**:

het ei	egg	**de eieren**
het kind	child	**de kinderen**
het lied	song	**de liederen**
het rund	cow	**de runderen**

Words ending in **-heid** form the plural with **-heden**:

de mogelijkheid	possibility	**de mogelijkheden**

Words originating in Latin might appear with their Latin or their Dutch plural ending:

de catalogus	catalogue	**de catalogi/catalogussen**
het museum	museum	**de musea/museums**

Exercise 7.1

Underline the plural forms.

Situation: Erik describes the neighborhood.

We wonen in een leuke buurt met huizen die bijna allemaal in de jaren 60 zijn gebouwd. De buurt heeft geen drukke straten, dus er zijn gelukkig weinig auto's. De meeste winkels zijn in de Raadhuisstraat, daar is ook het winkelcentrum met twee supermarkten. Het is een fantastische buurt voor kinderen, want er zijn twee parken vlakbij de school. De gemeente heeft er vorig jaar 50 nieuwe bomen geplant. Als je een film wilt zien, kun je kiezen uit twee bioscopen. Lekker eten kun je hier ook. Mijn favoriete restaurants zijn de pizzeria in de Raadhuistraat en het Indische restaurant op het Marktplein. Bij het sportcomplex zijn twee tennisbanen en vier voetbalvelden. Genoeg te doen dus!

Exercise 7.2

In this grocery list, which of the three plural forms is correct? Underline it.

1 een kilo tomaats/tomaaten/tomaten (singular = de tomaat)
2 een pond druiven/druifs/druifen (sg. = de druif)
3 twee zaken/zakken/zaaken (sg. = de zak) zoute drop
4 drie aubergines/aubergine's/auberginen (sg. = de aubergine)
5 twee meloens/meloen's/meloenen (sg. = de meloen)
6 twee poten/potten/pots (sg. = de pot) pindakaas
7 drie bekeren/beker's/bekers (sg. = de beker) vruchtenyoghurt
8 een zak bruine boons/bonen/boonen (sg. = de boon)

Exercise 7.3

Give the plural form for each word in brackets.

Situation: Description of Erik's interior.

Erik: Ons huis heeft drie (verdieping) _____ (1) met een woon- en eetkamer en een keuken beneden en drie (slaapkamer) _____ (2) boven. In de woonkamer staan twee (bank) _____ (3) met een paar groene (kussen) _____ (4) en een koffietafel en twee (bijzettafeltje) _____ (5). Er hangen witte (gordijn) _____ (6) voor de (raam) _____ (7) en er staan een paar moderne stalen (lamp) _____ (8). Rond

49

de eettafel staan zes (stoel) _____ (9). We hebben mooie (vloerkleed) _____ (10) op de grond en drie (boekenkast) _____ (11) tegen de muur.

Exercise 7.4

Give the plural form for the words in brackets.

Situation: Erik and Sanne discuss some household tasks for the day.

Sanne: Ik moet de (bed) _____ (1) afhalen, de (laken) _____ (2) wassen, de (vloer) _____ (3) stofzuigen en de (toilet) _____ (4) schoonmaken. Kun jij dan de (boodschap) _____ (5) even doen?

Erik: Goed, en ik zal ook even de (vuilnisbak) _____ (6) aan de straat zetten. Karin moet straks maar even de (aardappel) _____ (7) schillen. En laat Peter de (kattenbak) _____ (8) schoonmaken.

Sanne: Dat heb ik al gedaan. Maar hij kan de (hond) _____ (9) uitlaten. En hij moet ook even de lege (fles) _____ (10) naar de glasbak brengen.

Exercise 7.5

Give the plural form for the underlined words.

Situation: Sanne and her friend Julia discuss particularities of their diets. It turns out Julia has very bad habits.

Sanne

1 Drink je één <u>kopje</u> koffie per dag?

2 En 's avonds één <u>glas</u> wijn?

3 Rook je één <u>sigaret</u> na het eten?

4 En bij de tv één <u>zak</u> chips?

5 En bij het ontbijt één <u>ei</u>?

6 En bij de thee één <u>koekje</u>?

7 Bij de groente één <u>gehaktbal</u>?

Julia

Nee, ik drink wel acht _____ .

Nee joh, ik drink vier _____ .

Nee, ik rook drie _____, erg hè?

Nee, meestal eet ik twee _____ .

Ja, en op zondag twee _____ .

O nee, een heel pak _____ .

Eh, nou, liever twee _____ .

8 En bij de wijn meer dan één <u>pinda</u>?   Natuurlijk, een hand vol

                                                 _____ .

9 Eet je wel eens een <u>appel</u>?   De kinderen eten alle

                                                 _____ .

10 Maar toch wel eens een <u>banaan</u>?   Nee, ik lust geen

                                                 _____ .

Kind, wat eet je ongezond!!

UNIT EIGHT
Object pronouns

Introduction

This chapter introduces you to the *object* forms of the personal pronoun. As is the case with the subject forms, they can be used for persons as well as things.

Overview

Subject singular	Object singular	Subject plural	Object plural
ik	*mij/me*	wij/we	*ons*
jij/je, u	*jou/je, u*	jullie, u	*jullie, u*
hij, zij/ze, het/'t	*hem/'m, haar/d'r, het/'t*	zij/ze	*ze, hun, hen*

Examples in context

Waar is Maria? Ik zie *haar* niet.
Where is Maria? I don't see her.

Mijn broer is jarig. Ik geef *hem* een cd.
It's my brother's birthday. I'll give him a CD.

Geeft u *mij* maar een pond oude kaas.
Please give me a pound of mature cheese.

Ik zoek mijn sleutels. Ik had *ze* net nog.
I'm looking for my keys. I just had them.

De auto is vies. Ik moet *hem* wassen.
The car is dirty. I have to wash it.

Waar is je boek? Heb je *het* niet?
Where's your book? Don't you have it?

Notes

1 As is the case with the subject forms of the personal pronoun, the object forms have stressed and unstressed forms in the first, second, and third person singular. Whether to use the stressed or the unstressed form depends on context and intonation, i.e. what part of the sentence one wants to emphasize. In the sentence, for example, **Geef me even je** *pen*, the indirect object **me** is less important in the context than the object **pen**, and so **pen** is stressed. But in the sentence **Voor** *mij* **een pils, graag**, the speaker puts the emphasis on **mij** to distinguish him- or herself from the other guests in the group who might order something different. In general, the unstressed forms are used in speech and writing when the emphasis is not on the personal pronoun. The unstressed forms for the third person singular, **'m**, **d'r** (also **'r**) and **'t**, are mostly colloquial and more common in speech than in writing. The form **d'r** is only used for people, not for things.

2 The object form **hem** is used to refer to both people and things (**de**-words):

> **Dit is Henk. Ik speel tennis met** *hem*.
> This is Henk. I play tennis with him.

> **Heb jij een pen? Mag ik** *hem* **lenen?**
> Do you have a pen? May I borrow it?

When **hem** is used to refer to an object (not a person), it will never appear at the beginning of the sentence. In that case **hem** is replaced by **die**.

> **Hoe vind je de film? Ik vind** *hem* **goed. ~~Hem~~ vind ik goed.** ⇒ *Die* **vind ik goed.**

3 There are three object forms for the third person plural: **ze**, **hun**, **hen**.

   a The form **ze** is most common and can be used for both persons and things.

   > **Daar staan Joop en Mieke. Ik ga even met** *ze* **praten.**
   > Joop and Mieke are standing over there. I'm going to talk to them for a minute.

   > **Wat doe je met oude kranten? Ik doe** *ze* **in de recycling.**
   > What do you do with old newspapers? I put them in the recycling.

   At the beginning of a sentence, unstressed **ze** needs to be replaced with **die**:

   > *Die* **doe ik in de recycling.**

b The object form **hen** refers to persons as a direct object and is used after a preposition:

> **Ik heb *hen* gisteren opgebeld.**   I called them yesterday.
> **Ik heb een uur met *hen* gepraat.**   I talked to them for an hour.

In both these sentences, **hen** could be replaced by the unstressed form **ze**. However, when the object is emphasized, **ze** cannot be used. Note the difference between i and ii:

> i   **Hoe gaat het met je buren? O, ik praat niet meer met *ze*.**
> How are your neighbors? Oh, I don't talk to them anymore.
> ii   **Hoe gaat het met je buren? O, met *hen* praat ik niet meer.**

In sentence i, the spoken emphasis is on **praat**. In sentence ii, the spoken emphasis is on the object **hen** and **hen** can therefore not be replaced by **ze**.

c The form **hun** is used to refer to persons as indirect objects without a preposition.

> **Waar zijn de kinderen? Ik wil *hun* iets te drinken geven.**
> Where are the children? I want to give them something to drink.

> **Ik wil *hun* ook een verhaal vertellen.**
> I also want to tell them a story.

While there are specific grammatical rules for the use of **ze**, **hen** and **hun**, in speech the Dutch hardly distinguish anymore between **hen** and **hun**, and even in written language, **ze** has become quite common.

Exercise 8.1

Replace the subject or object of the question with an object pronoun in the answer.

1   Waar is het boek?   Ik zie _____ niet.
2   Heb jij de krant?   Nee, ik heb _____ niet.
3   Ruim je even de koffiekopjes op?   Nee, ik ruim _____ niet op!
4   Wie is die man?   Ik ken _____ niet.
5   Ken jij die vrouw?   Nee, ik ken _____ niet.
6   Weet je hoe laat het is?   Nee, ik weet _____ niet.
7   Speel je tennis met je buurman?   Nee, ik speel squash met

                                          _____ .
8   Vertel jij het nieuws aan opa en oma?   Nee, ik vertel het liever
                                          niet aan _____ .

9 Is die auto van jou of van mij?   Hij is van _____ samen.
10 Zijn die koekjes voor ons?   Ja, die heb ik voor _____
                                       gemaakt.

Exercise 8.2

In the following short dialogues, enter the correct object pronouns.

1 A: Voor wie is deze pizza?
   B: Die pizza is voor _____, dank u wel.
2 A: Dag mevrouw, wat kan ik voor _____ doen?
   B: Kunt u _____ vertellen waar de Rembrandtstraat is?
3 A: Zal ik een strippenkaart voor _____ kopen?
   B: Nee, dank je, ik heb al een strippenkaart gekocht.
4 A: Marja en Bas, is dat jullie huis?
   B: Ja, dat huis is van _____ .
5 A: Ga je vanavond naar Joop en Anke?
   B: Ja, ik ga met _____ naar de bioscoop.
6 A: Hoe vind je deze schoenen?
   B: Ik vind _____ niet zo mooi.
7 A: Ga je met ons mee naar een café?
   B: Nee, ik heb geen zin om met _____ mee te gaan.
8 A: Zijn deze sokken van mij of van _____ ?
   B: Dat zijn mijn sokken.
9 A: Is dit de trui van Peter?
   B: Nee, die is niet van _____, die is van Michael.
10 A: Mijn moeder is morgen jarig.
   B: O, wat leuk, wat geef je _____ ?

Exercise 8.3

Enter the object form of the personal pronoun.

*Situation: Erik's **Sinterklaas** shopping list.*

1 Peter heeft een nieuw tennisracket nodig, ja, ik geef _____ een racket.
2 Karin wil zo graag een paar nieuwe schaatsen, voor _____ koop ik
   schaatsen.
3 Sanne kookt al zo lang met oude pannen, _____ doe ik denk ik een groot
   plezier met een set nieuwe. En de oude pannen? Peter kan _____ nog
   gebruiken als hij gaat studeren.
4 Hm, wat zal Sanne _____ geven? Ik hoop dat ik een nieuwe boor
   krijg!

5 En de opa's en oma's? Voor _____ kunnen we wel een paar leuke boeken
   kopen.

Exercise 8.4

Replace the underlined noun (* = **het**-word) with an object pronoun.

Situation: Erik and the kids are getting ready for work and school and they can't find anything.

1 Erik: Sanne, heb jij <u>mijn leesbril</u> gezien?
   Sanne: Je hebt _____ op de keukentafel laten liggen.
2 Erik: Sanne, ik kan <u>mijn blauwe jasje</u>* niet vinden.
   Sanne: Je hebt _____ in de gangkast gehangen.
3 Peter: Mam, waar zijn <u>mijn gympen</u>? Ik heb _____ in de gymles nodig.
4 Sanne: Heb je _____ niet in je sporttas laten zitten?
5 Karin: Mam, ik zoek <u>mijn rode trui</u>. Heb je _____ in de was gestopt
           of zo?
6 Sanne: Nee, ik heb _____ in de kast gelegd, bij je andere truien.
7 Erik: Sanne, weet je dat <u>Joost en Joke</u> vanavond komen eten? Ik
           heb gisteren met _____ getelefoneerd.
8 Sanne: Wat?! Nee, dat weet <u>ik</u> niet. Waarom heb je _____ dat niet
           verteld?

Exercise 8.5

Enter the correct form of the personal pronoun. Note: It can be a subject or an object.

Situation: The Beumers are in a restaurant.

1 Erik: Jongens, wat willen _____ eten? Zeg het maar.
2 Peter: Nou, _____ heb wel zin in een kop tomatensoep. En daarna
           gegrilde kip.
3 Karin: _____ heb liever eerst een salade. En dan ook kip. Mam, wat
           neem _____?
4 Sanne: Een salade lijkt _____ heerlijk, ja. En de visschotel ook.
5 Ober: Wilt _____ bestellen? Zegt u _____ maar.
6 Erik: Voor _____ de tomatensoep en de kip. En voor _____ de salade
           en de kip.
7 Sanne: En voor _____ ook een salade en de visschotel.
8 Erik: En _____ neem de mosselen en de biefstuk.
9 Ober: Uitstekend, meneer. Wilt _____ misschien iets drinken?
10 Erik: Ja, kunt u _____ de wijnkaart brengen?

11 Ober: Natuurlijk, _____ komt eraan.
12 Erik: Zullen _____ een fles rode wijn bestellen? Of iets fris? Of witte wijn?
13 Peter: Het maakt _____ niet uit, pap. Ik neem een cola.
14 Karin: Ja, doe voor _____ ook maar een cola.
15 Sanne: Bestel dan voor _____ een glas rode en voor _____ een glas witte wijn.

UNIT NINE
Demonstrative pronouns

Introduction

In Dutch, demonstrative pronouns are called **aanwijzend voornaamwoord**; **aanwijzen** means to point to something. That is what they do, they point to something in particular. The form of the demonstrative pronoun depends on the gender of the noun, whether it is singular or plural, and how close or how far away the object is from the speaker.

Overview

	dichtbij close, **hier** here		**ver weg** far away, **daar** there	
de-words	*deze* **auto**	this car	*die* **auto**	that car
Plural	*deze* **auto's**	these cars	*die* **auto's**	those cars
het-words	*dit* **huis**	this house	*dat* **huis**	that house
Plural	*deze* **huizen**	these houses	*die* **huizen**	those houses

Examples in context

Wilt u *deze* vis of liever *die* vis?
Would you like this fish or rather that fish?

Zijn *deze* appels duurder dan *die*?
Are these apples more expensive than those?

Wat kost *dat* stuk kaas daar?
How much is that wedge of cheese over there?

***Dat* kost €3,95, mevrouw.**
That one is €3,95, madam.

You notice in the examples that the demonstrative pronoun can appear with or without the noun to which it refers, as long as it is clear what is meant. In the sentence **Zijn** *deze* **aardbeien duurder dan** *die*?, it is obvious that **aardbeien** is implied after *die*.

The demonstrative pronouns **die** and **dat** often replace a noun or a group of nouns (persons or things) that have been mentioned in an earlier context. In the following examples, the underlined parts are replaced with demonstrative pronouns.

Replacement with demonstrative

Waar is <u>Erik</u>**?**	*Die* **is in de bibliotheek** (library).
Komen <u>Erik en Sanne</u> **vanavond?**	**Nee,** *die* **komen niet.**
Van wie is <u>dit boek</u>**?**	*Dat* **is van mij.**
Waar zijn <u>mijn rode sokken</u> (red socks)**?**	*Die* **zitten in de wasmachine.**

Sometimes, the demonstrative pronoun **dat** refers to a complete sentence:

Wist je <u>**dat dit huis 200 jaar oud is**</u>**? Nee,** *dat* **wist ik niet.**
Did you know that this house is 200 years old? No, I didn't know that.

Note: Distance to an object isn't the only factor that determines the choice between **dit** or **dat**, **deze** or **die**. Distance in time can also play a role, or simply the order in which the speaker mentions two or more things. Examples:

We gaan *deze* **maand ons huis renoveren.**
We will renovate our house this month.

In *dat* **jaar lag er geen sneeuw.**
That year there wasn't any snow.

Herinner je je *die* **zomer in Italië?**
Do you remember that summer in Italy?

Ik vind *deze* **foto mooier dan** *die*.
I like this picture better than that one.

In this last example, the speaker's distance to the two pictures is irrelevant. He or she is probably close to both, but uses **deze** for the object mentioned first, and **die** for the object mentioned second.

Lastly, the demonstrative pronouns **dit** and **dat** can be used as preliminary subjects with verbs that link to the real subject of the sentence, usually a predicate noun or an adjective as a noun with verbs such as **zijn** 'to be', **worden** 'to become', **lijken** 'to appear'. Note: When the real subject is in the plural, the <u>linking verb</u> is also in the plural. Examples:

Dit is mijn broer Jan.

Dat is een goede film.

Dit wordt een leuke dag.

Dat lijkt wel een schildpad.

Dit <u>zijn</u> mijn ouders.

Dat <u>worden</u> later leuke jongens.

Dit is een mooie!

Dat <u>zijn</u> dikke!

This is my brother Jan.

That is a good movie.

This is going to be a nice day.

That looks like a turtle.

These are my parents.

They will become nice boys.

This is a beautiful one.

Those are fat!

Exercise 9.1

Circle the correct demonstrative pronoun (* = **het**-word).

Situation: Peter is working in his new weekend job in a restaurant. He's still getting used to the routine.

1 Baas: Hé Peter, breng die/dit broodje* even naar tafel 16!
2 Ober 2:   Peter, voor wie is deze/dat koffie?
3 Baas: Peter, deze/die mevrouw daar wacht op haar witte wijn!
4 Barman: Peter, hier zijn de biertjes voor dat/die mensen daar aan
             tafel 14.
5 Ober 3:   Peter, tafel 8, deze/dat is jouw tafel, niet mijn tafel!
6 Peter: Meneer, is deze/dit uitsmijter ('slice of bread with fried eggs
             on ham or veal') voor u?
7 Gast: Nee, dat/die is voor mijn vrouw.
8 Gast 2:   Ober, dit/deze soep is koud! Neem maar mee terug ('take
             it back').
9 Gast 3:   Ik wil betalen. Wanneer komt die/deze rekening ('bill',
             'check') nou?
10 Peter: Aaaaah! Dat/Dit werk is niks voor mij!

Exercise 9.2

Is the sentence correct or wrong, **goed** or **fout**?

Situation: Erik shows a family photo.

1 Deze is mijn vrouw Sanne.   goed – fout
2 Dit is mijn kinderen Peter en Karin.   goed – fout
3 Dat zijn de grootouders.   goed – fout
4 Dit is onze hond, hij heet Bruno.   goed – fout
5 Dit ben ik zelf, maar dat zie je wel.   goed – fout

Exercise 9.3

Enter the right pronoun: **die** or **dat** (* = **het**-word).

Situation: Sanne is doing the laundry. She is gathering items to be washed.

Sanne
1 Waar zijn je sokken van gisteren?

2 Moet ik je overhemd* wassen?

3 En je spijkerbroek?
4 Peter, waar zijn je sportkleren?
5 Karin, geef me even je ondergoed.*

Erik, Peter, Karin
_____ liggen nog onder het bed.

Nee, _____ heb ik pas één dag aan.

Ja, _____ is vies.
_____ zitten nog in m'n sporttas.
Ja, maar _____ mag niet in de was bij die stinksokken van Peter!

Exercise 9.4

Enter the right pronoun: **deze**, **die**, **dit** or **dat** (* = **het**-word, and (h) for **hier** indicates that the speaker is close, while (d) for **daar** indicates that the speaker is far away from the object).

Situation: Sanne is in a furniture store with her recently divorced friend who is shopping for her new flat.

Sanne
1 Vind je _____ bank (h) leuk?

2 Ja, dat is waar. En _____ bank (d)?

3 Bedoel je _____ zwarte tafeltje* (h)?

4 O, _____ (d) kost €395,-.

5 Ja, _____ (d) past echt bij jou!

Lydia
Ja, maar ik vind _____ kleur (d) lelijk.

Hm, gaat wel. Wat kost _____ tafeltje* (d)?

Nee, _____ witte (d) met _____ lampje* (d).

Wat duur! Vind je _____ lamp (h) mooi?

Ja! Maar ik wil _____ tafeltje (h) niet.

UNIT TEN
Possessive pronouns

Introduction

Possessive pronouns are used to indicate to whom an object belongs, as in **mijn huis** 'my house', **jouw auto** 'your car', **onze ouders** 'our parents' and so on. The official grammatical term is 'possessive adjective', but they are often reckoned among the different groups of pronouns, therefore, they shall be called 'possessive pronouns' here.

Overview

	Personal pronoun	Subject	Possessive pronoun	
Singular	**ik**	I	*mijn/m'n*[1]	my
	jij/je	you	*jouw/je*[2]	your
	u (formal)	you	*uw*	your
	hij, zij/ze, het	he, she, it	*zijn/z'n, haar/d'r*[3]	his, her
Plural	**wij, we**	we	*ons (het), onze (de)*[4]	our
	jullie	you	*jullie/je*[5]	your
	u (formal)	you	*uw*[6]	your
	zij/ze	they	*hun*	their

Notes

1 The first person possessive pronoun **mijn** has an unstressed or more colloquial form **m'n**. Instead of **Waar is mijn boek?** you might hear **Waar is m'n boek?** in everyday speech, and you will notice it written in literary language, for instance.
2 The second person possessive pronoun **jouw** is used only with emphasis, and the unstressed form **je** is much more common. Examples:

Dit is mijn boek. Waar is *jouw* boek?
This is my book. Where is *your* book?

In this sentence the stress is on **jouw** to emphasize the contrast with **mijn**.

Kees, waar is je *boek* vandaag?
Kees, where is your *book* today?

In this sentence, the stress is on **boek** because the speaker is emphasizing the object in question, the book, and not the person to whom it belongs.

3 The third person masculine possessive pronoun **zijn** has an unstressed form **z'n**, and the third person feminine possessive pronoun **haar** has an unstressed form **d'r**. Just like **m'n**, they are only used in more colloquial, informal speech. Examples:

Kees heeft *z'n* boek vandaag vergeten.
Kees has forgotten to bring his book today.

De lerares geeft *d'r* boek aan Kees.
The teacher gives her book to Kees.

Sometimes, in very informal speech, and generally not in written form, the informal **z'n** and **d'r** will appear after a name or a noun or a question word to express the possessive:

Erik *z'n* huis is mooi.	Erik's house is beautiful.
Sanne *d'r* fiets is kapot.	Sanne's bike is broken.
De hond *z'n* eten staat in de keuken.	The dog's food is in the kitchen.
Wie *z'n* koffie is dit?	Whose coffee is this?

4 The first person plural possessive pronoun appears in two forms: **ons** and **onze**. The form **ons** is used for **het**-words in the singular only. The form **onze** is used for **de**-words in the singular and all plural nouns. Examples:

het huis	*ons* **huis**	**de auto**	*onze* **auto**
de huizen	*onze* **huizen**	**de auto's**	*onze* **auto's**

5 The second person plural possessive pronoun can be **jullie** or **je**. The form **je** is used when two or more people are addressed and when the subject form **jullie** appears in the same sentence. Examples:

Peter en Karin, *jullie* brood is klaar.
Peter and Karin, your bread is ready.

Peter en Karin, nemen jullie *je* brood mee?
Peter and Karin, are you taking your bread with you?

6 The possessive pronoun for the second person formal is always **uw**, whether it is singular or plural. Examples:

Meneer, *uw* koffie komt eraan.
Sir, your coffee will be here in a minute.

Meneer, mevrouw, hier is *uw* sleutel.
Sir, madam, here is your key.

Lastly, the words **jouw** and **jou** are easily confused, because in spoken Dutch they don't differ in pronunciation. Remember that **jouw** is a possessive pronoun and **jou** is a personal pronoun, the object form of subject **jij, je**. Examples:

Ik heb dit boek voor *jou* gekocht.
I bought this book for you.

Ik heb dit boek voor *jouw* moeder gekocht.
I bought this book for your mother.

Exercise 10.1

Underline the <u>possessive pronouns</u> in the story.

Situation: Erik shows some family photos.

Dit is mijn familie. Hier zie je m'n vrouw Sanne en dat zijn onze kinderen Peter en Karin. Naast ons staan mijn ouders. Dit was hun 50-jarig huwelijksfeest. Mijn vader was toen al 80 jaar oud. Kijk, zijn broer staat ook op de foto, mijn oom Harm. Op deze foto hier zie je de familie van Sanne, haar ouders en haar broers en zussen met hun kinderen. En hier is een schoolfoto van Peter met z'n klasgenoten. Hun klasseleraar staat daar links. En deze foto is gemaakt na een volleybalwedstrijd van Karin. Hier staat ze met d'r hele team. En dit is een vakantiefoto van onze laatste reis naar Frankrijk. Mooi, hè?

Exercise 10.2

Enter the correct possessive pronoun.

Situation: Erik talks to grandma on the phone. She has many questions. Erik doesn't get a chance to answer.

Oma	Erik
1 Ha, Erik. Leuk dat je belt. Hoe gaat het op _____ werk?	...
2 Hoe is het met Sanne? Doet ze _____ yogalessen nog?	...
3 En Peter? Hoe zijn _____ cijfers op school?	...

4 Wanneer doet Karin _____ eindexamen?   . . .
5 Wanneer begint _____ vakantie? Gaan jullie weer naar
   Frankrijk?   . . .
6 Gaan de kinderen mee? Of hebben ze _____ eigen plannen? . . .
7 Kun je me deze week met _____ tuin helpen?   . . .
8 Breng je dan _____ grasmaaier mee? Die van mij is kapot. Hm!

Exercise 10.3

Enter the correct possessive pronoun.

Situation: Sanne is doing the laundry.

1 Sanne: Erik, waar is _____ overhemd van gisteren? Ik wil het wassen.
2 Erik: _____ overhemd? Kijk maar even in de slaapkamer. Daar ligt
           het.
3 Sanne: Kun je dan ook _____ nachtjapon ('night gown') even pakken?
4 Erik: Natuurlijk. Moeten _____ lakens ('sheets') ook met de was
           mee?
5 Sanne: Nee, die van de kinderen. Ik verschoon vandaag alleen _____
           bedden.
           Peter, Karin, breng _____ beddegoed ('bed sheets') even!

Exercise 10.4

Enter the right possessive pronoun.

Situation: Karin talks about her friends in her class.

_____ (1) beste vriendin heet Lydia. _____ (2) ouders hebben een zaak in
huishoudelijke artikelen. _____ (3) winkel is in het nieuwe winkelcentrum
in Noord. Verder doe ik veel met Ayshe en Yasmin. Ze zijn hier geboren,
maar _____ (4) ouders komen uit Turkije. _____ (5) klassenleraar is
meneer Hartman. Hij is echt gaaf, maar we lachen altijd om _____ (6) kleren.
Weet je wie _____ (7) favoriete jongen in de klas is? Joost! Ik mag altijd
achterop _____ (8) scooter zitten. Maar ik ben niet verliefd op hem, hoor!

Exercise 10.5

Enter the correct pronouns. Note: It isn't always a possessive pronoun.

*Situation: Peter is working in the restaurant. He is much more comfor-
table in his weekend job now.*

65

1 Gast 1:   Mag _____ bestellen?
2 Peter: Ik breng _____ zo even een menukaart.
3 Gast 2:   Ober, waar blijft _____ koffie?
4 Peter: _____ koffie komt eraan, meneer. Momentje.
5 Gast 3, 4:   Ober, bent u _____ rekening vergeten? _____ willen graag
               betalen.
6 Peter: Natuurlijk, hier is _____ rekening.
7 Ober 2:   Peter, kun _____ tafel 14 even nemen?
8 Peter: Geen probleem. Geef _____ even twee menukaarten,
               alsjeblieft.
9 Gast 5:   Ober, er zit een haar in _____ soep.
10 Peter: O, sorry mevrouw, _____ breng _____ een nieuw bord soep.

Ober, er zit een haar in mijn soep!

UNIT ELEVEN
Adjective endings

Introduction

Adjectives are used to describe nouns or pronouns: *a big house, a beautiful flower*. They can have two positions, before the noun: *a red car*, or after the noun: *the car is red*. If the adjective is before the noun, we call it an *attributive* adjective, if it follows the noun, it is a *predicate* adjective. In English, non-comparative adjectives don't change their form, regardless of their position and of the gender and number of the noun. But in Dutch they do change. This chapter introduces you to adjective endings.

Examples in context

Peter heeft een *grote* familie. Hij woont in een *groot* huis. De kamers in het huis zijn ook *groot*. Hij rijdt in een *grote* auto. Achter het *grote* huis ligt een *grote* tuin met twee *grote* vijvers. In de *grote* vijvers zwemmen *grote* vissen. Peter houdt van zijn *grote* familie en zijn *grote* huis.
Peter has a big family. He lives in a big house. The rooms in the house are big, too. He drives a big car. Behind the big house is a big garden with two big ponds. Big fish swim in the big ponds. Peter loves his big family and his big house.

Explanation

In the examples, you notice that the adjective **groot** appears in two forms: **grote** and **groot**. As a predicate adjective, the word **groot** stays the same: **het huis is groot, de garage is groot, de familie is groot, de vijvers zijn groot**. But as an attributive adjective, it is flexed most of the time and has the ending **-e**, except in one case. Overview:

	Definite		Indefinite	
Singular	**de grote auto**		Singular	**een grote auto**
	het grote huis			**een groot huis**
Plural	**de grote auto's**		Plural	**- grote auto's**
	de grote huizen			**- grote huizen**

Note: Only **het**-words (neuter nouns) used in the singular with the indefinite article **een** or in an otherwise indefinite context (with no article, with the negation **geen**, or after words such as **elk** 'each', **ieder** 'every', **welk** 'which', **veel** 'much', **weinig** 'little', **meer** 'more', **minder** 'less') are not flexed and thus do not get the ending **-e**. Examples:

Erik drinkt *koud* bier.
Erik drinks cold beer.

Erik drinkt geen *koud* bier.
Erik doesn't drink cold beer.

In de zomer drinkt Erik veel *koud* bier.
In summer Erik drinks a lot of cold beer.

In de winter drinkt Erik minder *koud* bier.
In summer Erik drinks less cold beer.

Attributive adjectives after *possessive pronouns* always have the ending **-e**, in singular and plural. See the overview for nouns in the singular:

de auto		**het huis**	
mijn grote auto	**onze grote auto**	**mijn grote huis**	**ons grote huis**
jouw/uw grote auto	**jullie grote auto**	**jouw/uw grote huis**	**jullie grote huis**
zijn/haar grote auto	**hun grote auto**	**zijn/haar grote huis**	**hun grote huis**

Attributive adjectives with *demonstrative pronouns* also always have the ending **-e**, in singular and plural.

de auto		**het huis**	
deze grote auto	**deze grote auto's**	**dit grote huis**	**deze grote huizen**
die grote auto	**die grote auto's**	**dat grote huis**	**die grote huizen**

Attributive adjectives before *indefinite non-countable **de**-nouns* have the ending **-e**, but attributive adjectives before *indefinite non-countable **het**-nouns* do not have the ending **-e**. See the examples in the table:

de koffie	coffee	*warme* **koffie**	warm coffee	*sterke* **koffie**	strong coffee
het water	water	*warm* **water**	warm water	*hoog* **water**	high water
de boter	butter	*romige* **boter**	creamy butter	*zoute* **boter**	salted butter
het brood	bread	*vers* **brood**	fresh bread	*oud* **brood**	old bread

Erik drinkt elke morgen een glas *koud* water en een kop *sterke* koffie.
Every morning Erik drinks a glass of cold water and a cup of strong coffee.

Adjectives that never get the ending -e

1 Some adjectives always end in **-en** and never change their form. A large group of these are adjectives that say something about the material of which an object is made. In Dutch, we call this group the **stofadjectieven**. Some examples:

het metaal	metal	*metalen*	het hout	wood	*houten*
het zilver	silver	*zilveren*	de wol	wool	*wollen*
het glas	glass	*glazen*	het brons	bronze	*bronzen*

Other examples: **het goud** 'gold' *gouden*, **het ijzer** 'iron' *ijzeren*, **het papier** 'paper' *papieren*, **de steen** 'stone' *stenen*, **het staal** 'steel' *stalen*, **het porcelein** 'porcelain' *porceleinen*, **het leer** 'leather' *leren*, **de zijde** 'silk' *zijden*, **het katoen** 'cotton' *katoenen*, **het marmer** 'marble' *marmeren*, **de stof** 'material' *stoffen*, **het fluweel** 'velvet' *fluwelen*.

However, **stofadjectieven** are only used before the noun, not as predicate adjectives. In the predicate position we use the word for the material with the preposition **van**. In English we say *a paper hat* but *a hat made out of paper*. Similarly in Dutch: **een *papieren* hoed**, but **een hoed *van papier***, as in the Dutch children's rhyme:

Eén, twee, drie, vier, hoedje van, hoedje van, één, twee, drie, vier, hoedje *van papier*.

Some adjectives of materials (mostly loan words) do not end in **-en** and also do not get the ending **-e**: **plastic**, **nylon**, **rayon**, **aluminium**, **platina**, **rubber**.

2 Past participles of irregular verbs used as an adjective that end in **-en**. Examples:

bakken	⇒	*gebakken* **aardappels** (baked or fried potatoes)
bederven	⇒	*bedorven* **eten** (spoilt food)
stelen	⇒	**het *gestolen* geld** (the stolen money)
verliezen	⇒	**de *verloren* armband** (the lost bracelet)

Note: Regular past participles used as an adjective *do* get the ending **-e**. Examples:

69

koken ⇒ het *gekookte* ei (the boilt egg)
versturen ⇒ *verstuurde* post (sent mail).

3 Some adjectives ending in **-en** such as **eigen** 'own', **verlegen** 'shy', **dronken** 'drunk', **open** 'open', **tevreden** 'satisfied', **volwassen** 'grown up', **even** 'even'. Examples:

Dit is een *verlegen* kind.
This is a shy child.

Ze gooiden de *dronken* man het café uit.
They threw the drunk out of the café.

In deze kolom staan *even* getallen.
This column lists even numbers.

A note on spelling in adjective declination

The rules discussed for verb conjugation and the formation of plural nouns apply here as well. Double vowels in a closed syllable become single in an open syllable, **-s** at the end of a word changes to **-z**, and **-f** changes to **-v** when the ending **-e** is added. Examples: **groot** ⇒ **grote** 'big', **laag** ⇒ **lage** 'low', **duur** ⇒ **dure** 'expensive', **vies** ⇒ **vieze** 'dirty', **boos** ⇒ **boze** 'angry', **lief** ⇒ **lieve** 'sweet', 'dear', **scheef** ⇒ **scheve** 'crooked', 'slanting'.

Exercise 11.1

In the text, underline only the predicate adjectives.

Situation: At the market.

Erik is op de markt. Hij heeft een grote boodschappentas bij zich. Zijn boodschappenlijst is lang. Hij loopt langs de kraam met verse groente. "Mooie asperges", denkt Erik, "maar ze zijn duur!" Hij koopt twee rode paprika's, drie kilo nieuwe aardappelen, een half pond middelgrote champignons en een grote doos aardbeien. De aardbeien zijn deze week goedkoop. "Pfff, wat is die tas nu zwaar."

Exercise 11.2

In the same text, now underline only the attributive adjectives.

Erik is op de markt. Hij heeft een grote boodschappentas bij zich. Zijn boodschappenlijst is lang. Hij loopt langs de kraam met verse groente.

"Mooie asperges", denkt Erik, "maar ze zijn duur!" Hij koopt twee rode paprika's, drie kilo nieuwe aardappelen, een half pond middelgrote champignons en een grote doos aardbeien. De aardbeien zijn deze week goedkoop. "Pfff, wat is die tas nu zwaar."

Exercise 11.3

Which one of the forms is correct? Underline or circle it. A star (*) indicates that the noun is a **het**-word.

Situation: Erik is tired from shopping and he's taking a break at a café. He's reading the lunch menu.

1 Salade met wit/witte bonen, tomaten, gekookt/gekookte eieren en zwart/zwarte olijven
2 Gazpacho (koud/koude tomatensoep met vers/verse groenten)
3 Boterham met twee gebakken/gebakkene eieren, ham en augurk
4 Kroket met Zaans/Zaanse mosterd op wit/witte of bruin/bruine brood*
5 Wit/Witte of bruin/bruine puntbroodje* met jong/jonge of oud/oude kaas
6 Risotto met courgette en gerookt/gerookte zalm
7 Gestoofd/Gestoofde kabeljauw met wit/witte wijnsaus
8 Warm/Warme appelgebak* met slagroom
9 Eigengemaakt/Eigengemaakte vanille-ijs* met warm/warme chocoladesaus
10 Grieks/Griekse yoghurt met vers/verse fruit*

Exercise 11.4

Combine the adjectives with the matching nouns and, when necessary, add the correct adjective ending. A star (*) indicates that the noun is a **het**-word. Choose from: **bruin, vers, mager, jong, zout, groot, wit, half, divers, vol**.

Situation: Sanne is reading the ads in the local newspaper looking for the special deals at the grocery store.

1 _____ kaas, per kilo deze week slechts €5,99!
2 Venco _____ drop, €2,99 per zak, twee halen, één betalen!
3 _____ rundergehakt*, nu €6,98 per pond.
4 Yoplait fruityoghurt, _____ soorten, nu €0,98 per bekertje.
5 Ariel wasmiddel, €7,98, nu het tweede pak voor de _____ prijs!
6 _____ brood*, gesneden, €1,98.
7 _____ wijn, huismerk, €5,99, twee voor een tientje! Meenemen!
8 Op = op!! Verkade chocolade, _____ assortiment*, nu 5 repen voor €6,95.
9 Maak een heerlijke café latte met Friesche Vlag _____ melk, 1 liter nu €1,98.
10 Alleen deze week! _____ spinazie, €0,98 per kilo. Koopje!

Exercise 11.5

Enter the correct form of the adjective. A star (*) indicates that the noun is a **het**-word.

Situation: Description of Erik and Sanne's house.

Erik heeft een (groot) _____ (1) huis* met een (mooi) _____ (2) tuin erachter. In het huis zijn vier (ruim) _____ (3) kamers met (groot) _____ (4) ramen. In de slaapkamer staan een (groot) _____ (5) bed*, een (modern) _____ (6) kast en twee (klein) _____ (7) nachtkastjes. Er staat een (leer) _____ (8) bank in de woonkamer. Sanne houdt van haar (antiek) _____ (9) koffietafel met de (zilver) _____ (10) kandelaars. Aan de werktafel staat een (duur) _____ (11) stoel en langs de wand drie (hoog) _____ (12) boekenkasten. Erik en Sanne koken op een (zwart) _____ (13) fornuis*. Naast het fornuis staat een (oud) _____ (14) koelkast. In de bijkeuken staat een (nieuw) _____ (15) wasmachine.

UNIT TWELVE
The adjective in comparison

Introduction

In English, when we compare objects (big–bigger–biggest), we use the endings **-er** and **-est**. For adjectives with more than one syllable (beautiful, important), we compare by using 'more' and 'most'. Here (and in some other aspects), Dutch differs from English.

The comparative and the superlative: overview and examples

Basic	Comparative: **(d)er**	Superlative: **st(e)**
mooi	**mooier**	**(het) mooist(e)**
leuk	**leuker**	**(het) leukst(e)**
groot	**groter**	**(het) grootst(e)**
duur	**duur**der	**(het) duurst(e)**

Eriks huis is groter *dan* het huis van zijn buurman, maar het huis van de buurman is mooier dan dat van Erik. Het grootste huis in de straat is het huis van de notaris. De auto van de notaris is kleiner dan die van Erik en zijn buurman, maar hij is wel het duurst(e), want het is een Ferrari!

Erik's house is bigger than his neighbor's house, but the neighbor's house is more beautiful than Erik's house. The biggest house on the street is the notary's house. The notary's car is smaller than that of Erik and that of Erik's neighbor, but it is the most expensive, because it is a Ferrari!

Predicate and attributive adjectives in comparison

Het huis van Jan is *groot.*
De auto van Jan is *duur.*

Het huis van de buurman is *groter.*
De auto van de buurman is *duurder.*

Het huis van de notaris is het *grootst(e).*
De auto van de notaris is *het duurst(e).*

Predicate adjectives in the comparative behave just like adjectives in their basic form. Predicate adjectives in the superlative, however, are always preceded by **het** ⇒ **Dit huis is** *het grootst(e).* **Die auto is** *het duurst(e).* The (**e**) is optional (mostly spoken).

Jan heeft een *groot* huis.
Jan heeft een *dure* auto.

De buurman heeft een *groter* huis.
De buurman heeft een *duurdere* auto.

De notaris heeft het *grootste* huis.
De notaris heeft de *duurste* auto.

Attributive adjectives in the comparative follow the same rules as attributive adjectives in their basic form. Attributive adjectives in the superlative always have the ending **-e** because they are never used with an indefinite meaning. It would be incorrect, therefore, to say **een duurste auto**.

Adjectives longer than one syllable

Adjectives that are longer than one syllable follow the same rules for the comparative and the superlative endings as one-syllable adjectives. Examples:

belangrijk	important	*belangrijker*	*(het) belangrijkst(e)*
interessant	interesting	*interessanter*	*(het) interessantst(e)*

Irregulars

Some adjectives have irregular forms for the comparative and the superlative.

goed	good	*beter*	*(het) best(e)*
veel	much	*meer*	*(het) meest(e)*
weinig	little, few	*minder*	*(het) minst(e)*
graag	gladly, willingly	*liever*	*(het) liefst(e)*

A few words on the meaning of **graag**. There is no easy or literal translation for this word. It is actually not an adjective, but an adverb, and can be added to any verb that expresses what one likes to do, eat, or drink. Examples:

Peter eet *graag* vis, maar hij eet *liever* vlees en hij eet *het liefst* sojaburgers.
Peter likes to eat fish, but he prefers meat, and his most favorite are soy patties.

Erik gaat *graag* naar de bioscoop, maar hij gaat *liever* naar een voetbalwedstrijd.
Erik likes to go to the movies, but he'd rather go to a soccer match.

Wat doe je *het liefst*?
What is your favorite activity?

Some notes on spelling

Note: Some of these spelling rules have been discussed in previous chapters.

1 Adjectives ending in **-r** receive an extra **-d-** in the comparative.

Examples: **duur** ⇒ **duurder, lekker** ⇒ **lekkerder, zwaar** ⇒ **zwaarder, ver** ⇒ **verder.**

2 An **-s** or **-f** at the end of an adjective changes to **-z-** or **-v-** in the comparative.

Examples: **boos** ⇒ **bozer, vies** ⇒ **viezer, lief** ⇒ **liever, gaaf** ⇒ **gaver.**

3 A double vowel in a closed syllable becomes single in an open syllable.

Examples: **groot** ⇒ **groter, laag** ⇒ **lager, breed** ⇒ **breder.**

4 A single consonant after a short vowel doubles in the comparative.

Examples: **dik** ⇒ **dikker, plat** ⇒ **platter, fel** ⇒ **feller, stom** ⇒ **stommer.**

5 Adjectives ending in **-s** form the superlative with **-t** rather than **-st**.

Examples: **vies** ⇒ **het viest, boos** ⇒ **het boost.**

75

Exercise 12.1

Change the adjective into <u>the comparative</u>: 1 **goed**, 2 **sterk**, 3 **veel**, 4 **zoet**, 5 **vet**, 6 **groot**, 7 **leuk**, 8 **lekker**, 9 **zacht**, 10 **lief**.

Situation: Peter and Karin like to visit oma, because everything is better than at home.

Bij oma is alles _____ (1) dan thuis. Oma maakt _____ (2) koffie dan mama. Je krijgt _____ (3) koekjes bij de koffie dan thuis. Oma's cake is _____ (4) dan thuis, want ze gebruikt meer suiker. Het vlees is _____ (5) dan thuis, want oma bakt het in de boter. Oma's televisie is _____ (6) dan de televisie thuis, en ze kijkt naar _____ (7) programma's. Het bier bij oma is _____ (8) dan thuis. De bedden zijn _____ (9) en Miepie, oma's poes, is _____ (10) dan Moppie, de poes thuis.

Exercise 12.2

Change the adjectives into <u>the superlative</u>.

Situation: Some facts about the Netherlands.

1 De (groot) _____ stad van Nederland is Amsterdam.
2 De (lang) _____ rivier van Nederland is de Linge, zij is 108 km lang.
3 De (hoog) _____ berg is op dit moment de Vaalserberg.
4 De (oud) _____ persoon van Nederland (in 2007) is 115 jaar oud.
5 De (veel) _____ bloemen komen uit Nederland.
6 Maar wat is het (goed) _____ bier?
7 En wat is de (lekker) _____ kaas?
8 En wie is de (populair) _____ popster?
9 En wie is de (snel) _____ voetbalspeler?
10 En wie is het (sympathiek) _____ lid van de koninklijke familie? Daarover denkt iedereen weer anders.

Exercise 12.3

Enter the correct form of the adjective. Note: It isn't always comparative or superlative.

Situation: Karin and Hetty talk about the boys in their class, specifically about their looks.

1 Karin: Joost heeft de (mooi) _____ ogen, vind je niet?
2 Hetty: Ja, maar hij heeft een (klein) _____ neus.
3 Karin: Klopt. Maar zijn neus is (groot) _____ dan die van Niko.
4 Hetty: Ja, en Niko heeft (veel) _____ puistjes dan Joost.
5 Karin: Martin draagt de (leuk) _____ kleren, vind ik.
6 Hetty: Ja, maar hij heeft een (stom) _____ bril!
7 Karin: Hoe vind jij dat (lang) _____ haar van Theo?
8 Hetty: Ja, hij heeft het (mooi) _____ haar van de hele klas!
9 Karin: Edo is (dik) _____ dan vorig jaar, vind je niet?
10 Hetty: Ja, maar hij eet ook de (veel) _____ hamburgers, haha.

Exercise 12.4

Look at the table and then fill in the blanks in the exercise.

Vragen aan vier studenten	Jan	Ina	Kees	Lydia
Hoe groot is je kamer?	24m^2	28m^2	15m^2	19m^2
Hoe vaak eet je pizza?	1/week	3/week	0	2/week
Hoeveel koffie drink je?	4 kopjes/ dag	1 kopje/ dag	geen	8 kopjes/ dag
Hoe vaak ga je naar de film?	3/mnd	4/mnd	0	1/mnd
Hoeveel sigaretten rook je?	0	5/dag	0	10/dag
Hoe vaak sport je?	2/week	4/week	elke dag	3/week
Hoelang studeer je per dag?	2 uur	3 uur	2 uur	4 uur
Hoe ver fiets je naar college?	2 km	6 km	1 km	10 km
Hoe oud ben je?	22	25	24	20

1 De kamer van Jan is _____ dan die van Ina maar _____ dan
   die van Kees en Lydia. Jan sport het _____ van allemaal. Hij drinkt
   _____ koffie dan Ina.
2 Ina's kamer is het _____. Ze rookt _____ dan Lydia. Ze
   studeert _____ dan Jan. Ze gaat het _____ naar de film. Ze
   is de _____.
3 Kees is een jaar _____ dan Ina en hij heeft de _____ kamer.
   Hij sport het _____. Hij studeert _____ dan Lydia en Ina.
   Zijn weg naar de universiteit is het _____. Ina fietst 5 km
   _____ dan Kees.
4 Lydia is de _____ en ze drinkt de _____ kopjes koffie van
   allemaal. Ze eet _____ pizza dan Ina. Ze rookt ook de
   _____ sigaretten. Ze studeert het _____. Ze gaat
   _____ vaak naar de film dan Ina. Zij woont het _____ van
   de universiteit.

UNIT THIRTEEN
Adverbs

Introduction

The function of an adverb in a sentence is to modify a verb, an adjective or another adverb. Adverbs give answers to questions such as how, when, how often, where, in what way or to what degree things happen. An adverb can be a single word or a group of words, in which case it is easier to think of it as an adverbial phrase. A particularly interesting but difficult group of adverbs are the *particles*, adverbs that give a certain attitude or emotion (judgement) to an expression. They are widely used in colloquial Dutch, and it takes time for the learner to develop a feeling for when to use which particle. A small section will be devoted to some of the particles here, and they will return in more detail in Chapter 20 on the imperative, the command form.

Examples in context

> **Peter, de zoon van Erik, speelt *goed* voetbal. Hij speelt *regelmatig* een wedstrijd. Erik gaat *altijd* kijken. *Vandaag* speelt het voetbalteam van Peter *thuis*. De wedstrijd is *heel* spannend. Na de wedstrijd drinken de jongens *samen* met hun fans een cola of biertje in de kantine.**
> Peter, Erik's son, plays soccer *well*. He *regularly* plays matches. Erik *always* goes to watch. *Today*, Peter's team is playing a *home* game. The game is *very* exciting. After the game, *together* with their fans, the boys have a coke or a beer in the canteen.

The words in italic each fulfill one of the functions in the introduction. The adverb **goed** answers the question: how?, **regelmatig** and **altijd** answer the question: how often?, **vandaag** answers the question: when?, **thuis** answers the question: where?, **heel** gives an answer to the question: to what degree?, and **samen** also answers the question: how?, in what way?

Adjectives as adverbs

In the example **Peter speelt goed voetbal, goed** is an adjective used as an adverb. When used as an adverb, the adjective remains uninflected, it doesn't get the ending **-e**. But as adverbs, such words do have endings in the comparative and the superlative. Examples:

> **Peter speelt *goed* voetbal, maar Johan speelt *beter.***
> Peter plays soccer well, but Johan plays better.

> **Karin en Lydia fietsen *snel*, maar Erika fietst *het snelst(e).***
> Karin and Lydia bike fast, but Erika bikes fastest.

True adverbs

Next, we discuss adverbs of place and direction, adverbs of time and frequence, adverbs of manner, modality and degree. The last section of this chapter is devoted to particles.

Adverbs of place and direction

thuis	at home	**naar huis**	(to) home
binnen	inside	**buiten**	outside
ergens	somewhere	**nergens**	nowhere
overal	everywhere	**naartoe**	to
beneden	downstairs	**boven**	upstairs
daar	there	**hier**	here
linksaf	to the left	**rechtsaf**	to the right
heen	to	**vandaan**	from

These are some commonly used adverbs of place. Some can be combined with the preposition **naar** to change from location to direction: **naar beneden** 'going downstairs', **naar boven** 'going upstairs', **naar binnen** 'going inside', **naar buiten** 'going outside'. Others are combined with **heen** or **naartoe** to do that: **ergens heen** 'going somewhere', **nergens heen** 'going nowhere', **ergens naartoe, nergens naartoe, hierheen, hiernaartoe** 'coming here', **daarheen, daarnaartoe** 'going there'. The adverb **vandaan** can be combined with others to express motion from somewhere: **overal vandaan** 'from everywhere', **ergens vandaan** 'from somewhere', **nergens vandaan** 'from nowhere', **hiervandaan** 'from here', **daarvandaan** 'from there'. The adverbs **naartoe, heen** and **vandaan** are combined with **waar** to make question words: **waarnaartoe** 'where to?' **waarheen** 'where to?' and

waarvandaan 'from where?'. In sentence format, they are often separated. Examples:

Waar komt u *vandaan?*	Where are you from?
Parijs? *Daar* ben ik nog nooit *naartoe* geweest.	Paris? I have never been there.
Ik wil *daar* graag eens *heen.*	I would like to go there some day.
De voetbalfans kwamen *overal vandaan.*	The soccer fans came from everywhere.

Adverbs of time and frequence

Many of these have been introduced in Unit 5. This is a brief overview of the most commonly used adverbs.

1 Parts of the week: **vandaag, morgen, overmorgen, gisteren, eergisteren.**
2 Order of events: **eerst, dan, daarna, vervolgens, verder, tenslotte.**
3 Frequency: **altijd, meestal, vaak, regelmatig, soms, zelden, nooit.** Also: **telkens** 'repeatedly', **aldoor** 'all the time', **steeds** 'repeatedly', 'continuously'.
4 Adverbs of time that are difficult to summarize under one category:

nu, thans	now	**nog**	still
eens	some day	**ooit**	some day
gauw	soon, quickly	**binnenkort**	soon
even	for a minute	**meteen**	immediately
ineens	suddenly	**plotseling**	suddenly
vroeg	early	**laat**	late
pas	recently, only	**dadelijk**	right away
al	already	**net**	just
straks	later	**zo**	in a minute/second
eindelijk	finally	**weer**	again

The usual position of the adverb is right after the verb or at the beginning of the sentence. If it is at the beginning of the sentence, there is *no* comma after the adverb, and subject and verb are inverted. Examples:

De kinderen gaan *vandaag* naar het strand.	The kids will go to the beach today.
Ze moeten *vroeg* vertrekken.	They have to leave early.
Vandaag heeft Erik een vergadering.	Today, Erik has a meeting.
Erik gaat *eerst* naar de vergadering.	First, Erik goes to the meeting.
Daarna gaat hij boodschappen doen.	Afterwards, he's going grocery shopping.

Pay attention to the two meanings of **pas**: 'recently', 'only', 'not until':

1 **We hebben** *pas* **een huis gekocht.**
We recently bought a house.

2 **We kopen** *pas* **een huis als we het kunnen betalen.**
We will not buy a house until we can pay for it.

Lastly, the adverbs **meer** or **weer** can be added to some of the adverbs of time to express a sense of finality or continuation. Similarly, **nog** can be combined with some adverbs to slightly alter the meaning. Examples of such combinations are: **nooit meer** 'not ever anymore', **nooit weer** 'never again', **alweer** 'already again', **nog nooit** 'not yet ever', **nog even** 'for a little while more', **nog net** 'just barely', **pas nog** 'only recently'.

Ik wil hem *nooit meer* **zien.**	I don't want to see him ever again.
Zul je dat *nooit weer* **doen?**	Promise to never do that again.
Ben je daar nu *alweer*?	Is that you again (so soon)?
Hij is *nog nooit* **in Parijs geweest.**	He has never (ever) been in Paris.
Ach, blijf *nog even* **een kop thee drinken.**	Come, stay a bit longer for a cup of tea.
Ik heb het examen *nog net* **gehaald.**	I just barely passed the test.
Ik heb Jan *pas nog* **gezien.**	I just recently saw Jan.

Adverbs of manner, modality and degree

These adverbs answer the questions how, in what way, to what degree or to what extent something happens. There are quite a few, and therefore the following is an attempt to give a brief overview of the most frequently used adverbs. Firstly, many adjectives can be used as *adverbs of manner*:

leuk	nicely	**mooi**	beautifully
goed	well	**slecht**	badly
snel	quickly, fast	**langzaam**	slowly
stom	stupidly	**boos**	angrily

Zij zingt *mooi*.	She sings beautifully.
Jan keek *boos* **naar mij.**	Jan looked at me angrily.
De voetballer speelt *slecht*.	The soccer player plays badly.

Next, *adverbs of modality* express the reality value of what is stated in the sentence. They express the speaker's attitude to what he or she says. Such adverbs are:

misschien/wellicht	perhaps	**natuurlijk**	of course
helaas	unfortunately	**gelukkig**	fortunately
mogelijk	possibly	**inderdaad**	indeed
duidelijk	obviously, clearly	**zeker**	surely
eigenlijk	actually	**echt**	really
hopelijk	hopefully	**blijkbaar**	apparently
waarschijnlijk	probably	**schijnbaar**	as it seems
ongetwijfeld	undoubtedly		

Het gaat vanavond *waarschijnlijk* regenen.
It's probably going to rain tonight.

Het heeft gisteren *inderdaad* geregend.
It really did rain yesterday.

De straten zijn nat. *Blijkbaar* heeft het geregend. *Gelukkig* regent het nu niet meer.
The streets are wet. Apparently it rained. Fortunately it isn't raining anymore.

Deze schoenen zijn *echt* mooi. Wat kosten ze *eigenlijk*?
These shoes are really beautiful. By the way, how much are they?

89 euro? Dat is *helaas* te duur voor mij.
89 euros? Too bad, that's too expensive for me.

And lastly, *adverbs of degree* express the degree or intensity of an adjective, another adverb or a verb phrase. A number of these are *quantifying* adverbs.

zeer	very	**heel**	very
echt	really	**nogal**	somewhat
ook	also	**te**	too
helemaal	entirely	**totaal**	totally
nauwelijks	hardly	**vrijwel**	pretty much
erg	very (badly)	**hartstikke**	very
vrij	rather	**redelijk**	reasonably
zo	so, very	**absoluut**	absolutely
volkomen	totally	**volledig**	totally
bijna	almost	**genoeg**	enough

Ik vind dit schilderij *hartstikke* mooi. I find this painting very very beautiful.

This adverb puts special emphasis on the adjective **mooi**.

Jan speelt *redelijk* goed tennis.   Jan plays tennis reasonably well.

This adverb modifies the other adverb **goed**.

Ik had mijn boek *bijna* vergeten.   I almost forgot my book.

This adverb modifies the verb.

The adverb graag

This adverb can be added to verbs that talk about food, drink or any activity in which the subject or the object of the enunciation is involved. It can appear in the comparative form **liever** or the superlative form **het liefst** to express a degree of preference. Examples:

Erik speelt *graag* voetbal, maar hij gaat *liever* tennissen en hij zwemt *het liefst*.
Erik likes to play soccer, but he prefers to play tennis and he most likes to swim.

Erik eet *graag* pizza, maar hij eet *liever* een kebab en *het liefst* een gewone gehaktbal.
Erik likes to eat pizza, but he prefers kebab and his favorite is a plain old meatball.

Erik eet het liefst een gewone gehaktbal.

Particles

In Dutch, these adverbs are also called **oordeelspartikels**, particles of judge-ment, because they give a certain emotional or judgmental flavor to the speaker's statement. They are particularly meaningful in the imperative, the command form, which will be discussed in Chapter 20. Some of the most commonly used particles are: **even, eens, maar, alleen, toch, zelfs, nou, dan, al**. It is very difficult to give exact English translations for these adverbs, because their meaning can change depending on context and intonation. Another reason why they are difficult to translate is that often they do not appear alone, but in combination with another particle. A few examples:

Mia:	**Zijn er *nog* witte asperges?**	Do you still have white aspara-gus?
Verkoper:	**Ik zal *even* voor u kijken.**	Sales person: I'll go and have a look for you.

The particle **even** implies that it will not take long and that it isn't too much of an effort for the sales person. It makes the statement casual and friendly.

Erik:	**Komen Wim en Ineke vanavond?**	Are Wim and Ineke coming tonight?
Sanne:	**Ja, dat heb ik je gisteren *toch* verteld!**	Yes, didn't I tell you yesterday?

The particle **toch** in this context implies that the speaker is a bit annoyed that the other speaker doesn't remember something she has told him before.

Erik tegen Sanne: Goh zeg, het is *al* tien over twaalf.
Erik to Sanne: Wow, it is ten past twelve already.

Wim tegen Ineke: Ja, we gaan *maar eens*.
Wim to Ineke: Yes, we should be going. (literally: We will just go.)

The adverb combination **maar eens** doesn't literally translate into English but it implies that the speaker is more or less resigned to the fact that he or she should do something.

There are many ways to use particles and particle combinations, too many to discuss here in detail. More examples can be found in Unit 20.

Exercise 13.1

Underline the adverbs and particles in the dialogues:

Persoon A	Persoon B
1 Hoe is dat nieuwe boek van 't Hart?	Het is heel goed!
2 Ik wil graag een kop koffie.	Ik kom dadelijk bij u, meneer.
3 Wanneer gaan we eigenlijk zwemmen?	Vanmiddag, dat weet je toch!
4 Die vrouw zingt mooi, hè?	Nee, het klinkt vreselijk!
5 Kun je me even helpen?	Nee, ik heb nu echt geen tijd.

Exercise 13.2

Is the underlined word an adjective or an adverb?

1 Karin speelt mooi piano.   adjective – adverb
2 Erik tennist redelijk goed.   adjective – adverb
3 De yogalessen van Sanne zijn leuk.   adjective – adverb
4 Peter traint hard voor zijn voetbalteam.   adjective – adverb
5 Pianolessen zijn duurder dan yogalessen.   adjective – adverb

Exercise 13.3

Where does the adverb fit in? Rewrite the sentence beginning with the subject.

Example: (waarschijnlijk) Jan komt naar het feest. → Jan komt waarschijnlijk naar het feest.

1 (zaterdag) Erik wil naar de voetbalwedstrijd.

_____

2 (compleet) De kaarten voor de voetbalwedstrijd zijn uitverkocht.

_____

3 (heel) Erik vindt het jammer. (graag) Hij wil de wedstrijd zien.

_____

4 (meteen) 'Ik bestel kaarten voor volgende week,' zegt Erik.

_____

5 (ook) 'Sorry, meneer, maar die wedstrijd is uitverkocht.'

_____

Exercise 13.4

In this exercise, place the adverb at the beginning of the sentence, and
remember to use the correct word order.

1 Sanne gaat naar de yogales (straks).

_____

2 Na de yogales gaat ze met Hester koffiedrinken (misschien).

_____

3 Hester heeft tijd (hopelijk).

_____

4 Het is mooi weer (gelukkig).

_____

5 Ze kunnen buiten op een terras zitten (dan).

_____

Exercise 13.5

Enter the correct adverb. Select from: **hartstikke**, **heel**, **misschien**, **bijna**,
eindelijk, **al**, **vrij**, **helaas**, **ook**, **net**.

Een nieuwe flat voor Cindy

_Situation: Cindy writes an email to her parents to let them know she just
got a new apartment._

Hoi pap en mam,
Ik heb _____ (1) een nieuwe flat, na zes maanden zoeken! Ik heb
_____ (2) met de verhuurder getelefoneerd. Morgen krijg ik de sleutel _____ (3) en ik ga op 10 juli verhuizen. De flat is _____ (4)
groot, rond 80 vierkante meter, dus dat is niet zo slecht. De keuken is
_____ (5) klein, er is geen plaats voor een eettafel, maar die past
prima in de woonkamer. De badkamer is _____ (6) klein, maar groot
genoeg voor mij. Ik ben _____ (7) klaar met inpakken, maar Mark
is _____ (8) op 10 juli op vakantie. Kunnen jullie me _____ (9)
helpen met verhuizen? Ik ben _____ (10) blij met m'n nieuwe flat.
Groetjes, Cindy

UNIT FOURTEEN
The adverb **er**

Introduction

The adverb **er** needs its own chapter. It often appears in Dutch sentences, and it can have many different meanings. This chapter gives an introduction to the functions of **er** in combination with an indefinite subject, as a place indicator, and, in combination with a cardinal number, as an indicator of quantity.

Examples

Er is een stad in Nederland die Amsterdam heet. Het is de grootste stad van Nederland. *Er* wonen bijna 745.000 mensen. *Er* komen veel toeristen naar Amsterdam. Je kunt *er* veel museums en andere toeristische attracties bezoeken. Denk je dat Venetië veel bruggen heeft? De binnenstad van Amsterdam heeft *er* meer dan 250.

There is a city in the Netherlands called Amsterdam. It is the largest city in the Netherlands. Almost 745 000 people live there. Many tourists come to Amsterdam. You can visit many museums and other tourist attractions there. Do you think Venice has many bridges? The inner city of Amsterdam has more than 250 (of them).

Indefinite subject

The function of **er** in these sentences is to announce the subject while the actual *word for the subject* follows later in the sentence. Examples:

Er is *een museum* op de Prinsengracht.
There is a museum on Prinsengracht.

Er zijn *heel veel bruggen* in Amsterdam.
There are very many bridges in Amsterdam.

With the verb **zijn**, 'to be', **er** simply indicates that something exists. Therefore, this function of **er** is also called 'existential'. It is similar to English 'there is', 'there are'. In the same way, as a preliminary subject, **er** can also be combined with other verbs. Examples:

Er liggen *woonboten* in de gracht.	There are houseboats on the canal.
Er gaan *veel toeristen* naar Amsterdam.	Many tourists go to Amsterdam.

The adverb **er** can only be used in this way when the subject is indefinite, i.e. with an indefinite article, without an article, with a number, or with indefinite pronouns. Examples:

Er is *iemand* in de woonboot.	There is someone in the houseboat.
Er zit *niemand* in het café.	There is nobody in the café.
Er staat *iets* over Anne Frank in de krant.	There is something about Anne Frank in the paper.
Er is vandaag *niets* te doen in de stad.	There is nothing to do in town today.

And lastly, with question words such as **wie, wat, welke/wat voor, hoeveel**:

Wie is *er* aan de beurt?	Whose turn is it?
Wat zit *er* in de soep?	What is in the soup?
Welke meubels staan *er* in de kamer?	Which pieces of furniture are in the room?
Hoeveel appels zitten *er* in de taart?	How many apples are in the cake?

Place indicator

Amsterdam is een leuke stad. Ik ben *er* vaak geweest. Je kunt *er* veel museums bezoeken. Het is een leuke stad om te winkelen. Ik heb *er* dit antieke vaasje gekocht. Je kunt *er* ook heel lekker eten.
Amsterdam is a nice city. I have often been there. You can visit many museums there. It is also a nice city for shopping. I bought this antique vase there. You can also eat very well there.

As a place indicator, **er** works the same way as unstressed **daar**. It refers to a place that has been mentioned before and is therefore known to the listener. Similarly, it can refer to a place that may not have been mentioned but that is expected to be known:

Is Kees *er* vandaag niet?   Is Kees not here today?
Kijk, de bus staat *er* al.   Look, the bus is already here.

In this function, **er** is never emphasized or stressed. It can therefore not be at the beginning of the sentence. Most of the time, it follows the verb. If one wanted to use emphasis, the adverb **er** must be replaced with **daar** or **hier**. The adverbs **daar** and **hier** can be at the beginning of the sentence or after the verb. Examples:

Amsterdam? *Daar* ben ik nog nooit geweest.
Amsterdam? I've never been there.

Waar is Kees? *Hier* is hij niet.
Where's Kees? He isn't here.

Er is een Indisch restaurant in Utrecht. Ik heb *daar* een keer heel goed gegeten.
There is an Indian restaurant in Utrecht. I had a really good meal there once.

With a number

The adverb **er** replaces a noun when a number indicates a quantity of said noun. It would be overkill to answer the question **Hoeveel eieren hebben we nodig?** 'How many eggs do we need?' with **We hebben zes eieren nodig.** We know we are talking about eggs, and therefore it is sufficient to answer: **We hebben *er* zes nodig.** More examples:

Hoeveel kinderen heeft Erik? Hij heeft *er* twee.
How many children does Erik have? He has two (of them).

Hoeveel boterhammen eet Peter? Hij eet *er* zes.
How many slices of bread does Peter eat? He eats six (of them).

This happens not only when a cardinal number is used to indicate quantity, but also with indefinite cardinal numbers such as **veel** 'much', 'many', **een paar** 'a couple', 'a few', **geen** 'none', **genoeg**, **voldoende** 'enough', 'sufficient'. Examples:

Hoeveel tennisrackets heeft Erik? Hij heeft *er* een paar.
How many tennis rackets does Erik have? He has a couple.

Hoeveel koekjes eet Peter? Hij eet *er* veel.
How many cookies does Peter eat? He eats a lot.

Heeft de groenteman vandaag asperges? Nee, hij heeft _er_ geen.
Does the greengrocer have asparagus today? No, he doesn't have any.

For more uses of **er**, see the corresponding unit in _Intermediate Dutch_.

Exercise 14.1

In each first sentence, underline the word that is replaced by **er** in the second.

1 Erik woont in Hardegarijp. Hij werkt er ook.
2 Erik heeft twee tennisrackets. Hij gebruikt er één.
3 Sanne houdt van haar yogales. Ze gaat er twee keer per week heen.
4 Karin neemt elke dag twee koeken mee naar school. Ze geeft er één aan Lydia.
5 Bij Eriks huis is een grote achtertuin. Je kunt er heerlijk in de zon zitten.

Exercise 14.2

Put the words in the correct order to make complete sentences.

1 nieuwe – is – op – kraam – Er – een – markt – de

_____

2 kopen – er – brood – kunt – allerlei – Je – soorten

_____

3 altijd – Sanne – harde – koopt – er – broodjes

_____

4 in – staat – leuke – kraam – Er – een – de – verkoper

_____

5a voor – Sanne – broodjes – betaalt – acht

_____

5b tien – krijgt – maar – zij – er

_____

Exercise 14.3

Answer the questions using **er** as an indicator of quantity.

Situation: Erik's eating habits.

1 Hoeveel kopjes koffie drinkt Erik per dag? (vier)

2 Hoeveel koekjes eet hij bij de koffie? (geen)

_____

3 Hoeveel plakken kaas doet hij op zijn brood? (twee)

_____

4 Hoeveel aardappels eet hij bij de gehaktbal? (zes)

_____

5 Hoeveel flesjes bier drinkt hij op een feestje? (veel)

_____

Exercise 14.4

What was the question of the guest to the waiter?

1 _____?
   Ober: Ja, er zit vlees in de soep.
2 _____?
   Ober: Nee, er zitten geen champignons in de saus.
3 _____?
   Ober: Er zitten tomaten, olijven, kaas en tonijn op de pizza.
4 _____?
   Ober: Nee, er is geen lasagne meer.
5 _____ asbakken?
   Ober: Nee, die zijn er niet, want u mag hier niet roken!

Exercise 14.5

Speaking exercise. Answer the questions using **er** to replace the underlined object.

1 Ben je ooit in Parijs geweest?
2 Heb je wel eens in een bar gewerkt?
3 Studeer je veel in de bibliotheek?
4 Mag je in de trein roken?
5 Hoe vind je het in Amsterdam?
6 Hoeveel fietsen heb je?
7 Hoeveel boeken lees je per maand?
8 Hoeveel pizza's eet je per week?
9 Hoeveel films zie je per maand?
10 Hoeveel mensen ken je in Nederland?

UNIT FIFTEEN
Negatives

Introduction

The adverb **niet** 'not' is most commonly used to make sentences and sentence parts negative in Dutch. In some cases, however, we use the negative indefinite article **geen** 'no'. The main focus points of this chapter are the difference between **niet** and **geen** and the position of **niet** in the sentence.

Examples

Erik komt uit Nederland. Hij is advocaat. Hij woont in Hardegarijp. Hij is getrouwd met Sanne. Hij heeft twee kinderen, Karin en Peter. Erik houdt van voetbal.
Erik is from the Netherlands. He is a lawyer. He lives in Hardegarijp. He is married to Sanne. He has two children, Karin and Peter. Erik likes soccer.

Josh komt *niet* uit Nederland. Hij is *geen* advocaat. Hij woont *niet* in Hardegarijp. Hij is *niet* getrouwd. Hij heeft *geen* kinderen. Hij houdt *niet* van voetbal.

So when do you say **niet** and when do you say **geen**?

Josh is not from the Netherlands. He is not a lawyer. He doesn't live in Hardegarijp. He is not married. He doesn't have any children. He doesn't like soccer.

The word **geen** is used to negate a noun with an indefinite article (**een**) or no article (Ø).

Erik is Ø advocaat.	**Josh is *geen* advocaat.**
Erik is a lawyer.	Josh is not a lawyer.
Erik heeft Ø kinderen.	**Josh heeft *geen* kinderen.**
Erik has children.	Josh has no children.
Erik spreekt Ø Nederlands.	**Josh spreekt *geen* Nederlands.**
Erik speaks Dutch.	Josh doesn't speak Dutch.
Erik heeft *een* vrouw.	**Josh heeft *geen* vrouw.**
Erik has a wife.	Josh has no wife.

The word **niet** is used to negate everything else. This includes verbs, adjectives and adverbs, prepositional phrases, time expressions, nouns with definite articles (**de**, **het**), demonstrative pronouns (**deze**, **die**, **dit**, **dat**) and possessives, and the words **er**, **daar** and **hier**.

The position of niet in the sentence

The adverb **niet** follows

1	the conjugated verb	**Erik werkt *niet*.**
		Erik doesn't work (isn't working).
2	a time expression	**Erik werkt vandaag *niet*.**
		Erik doesn't work (isn't working) today.
3	the definite object	**Erik koopt het huis *niet*.**
		Erik doesn't buy (isn't buying) the house.
4	**er, daar, hier**	**Erik is er *niet*.**
		Erik isn't here.

Note: Sometimes **niet** doesn't follow these rules exactly. Depending on what you want to negate and what you emphasize, **niet** may have a different position. Note the difference in emphasis in the following examples:

Erik werkt vandaag *niet*.
Erik doesn't work (isn't working) today.

Erik werkt niet *vandaag*, maar *morgen*.
Erik isn't working today, but he is tomorrow.

Deze bus rijdt op zaterdag *niet*.
This bus doesn't run on Saturdays.

Deze bus rijdt niet op *zaterdag*, maar op *zondag*.
This bus doesn't run on Saturdays, but it does on Sundays.

Erik eet de pizza *niet*.
Erik doesn't eat (isn't eating) the pizza.

Erik eet niet *de pizza*, maar *de soep*.
Erik doesn't eat (isn't eating) the pizza, but the soup.

Erik is niet *hier*, maar *daar*.
Erik isn't here, but (he is) there.

The adverb **niet** precedes:

1	a prepositional phrase	**Erik werkt *niet* in een café.**
		Erik doesn't work in a café.
2	an adverb or adjective	**Erik speelt *niet* goed voetbal.**
		Erik doesn't play soccer well.
3	a predicate adjective	**Erik is *niet* dik.**
		Erik isn't fat.

Examples to compare:

1a The negation of **Erik drinkt koffie** 'Erik drinks coffee' is **Erik drinkt *geen* koffie** 'Erik doesn't drink coffee' because **koffie** is an *indefinite object*.
1b The negation of **Erik drinkt de koffie** 'Erik drinks the coffee' is **Erik drinkt de koffie *niet*** because **de koffie** is a *definite object*.
2a The negation of **Erik vindt de koffie lekker** 'Erik thinks the coffee is delicious' is **Erik vindt de koffie *niet* lekker** 'Erik doesn't think the coffee is delicious' because in this sentence the *predicate adjective* is negated.
2b The negation of **Dit is lekkere koffie** 'This is delicious coffee' is **Dit is *geen* lekkere koffie** 'This coffee is not delicious' because the negated sentence part is an *indefinite subject* with an attributive adjective.

It is important, therefore, to check whether the subject or object of the sentence is definite or indefinite.

The adverbs nog and meer in negation

We often see the adverbs **nog** and **meer** in combination with **niet** or **geen**, for example to contrast the adverbs **al** and **nog**.

A: **Is de supermarkt** *al* **open?**	B: **Nee, de supermarkt is** *nog niet* **open.**	The adverb **wel**

A: **Is de supermarkt** *al* **open?**
A: Has the supermarket opened yet?

B: **Nee, de supermarkt is** *nog niet* **open.**
B: No, the supermarket hasn't opened yet.

A: **Heb je** *al* **brood gekocht?**
A: Have you bought bread yet?

B: **Nee, ik heb** *nog geen* **brood gekocht.**
B: No, I haven't bought bread yet.

A: **Is er** *nog* **koffie?**
A: Is there any coffee left?

B: **Nee, er is** *geen* **koffie** *meer*.
B: No, there is no more coffee.

A: **Woont Erik hier** *nog*?
A: Does Erik still live here?

B: **Nee, die woont hier** *niet meer*.
B: No, he doesn't live here anymore.

The adverb wel

The adverb **wel** is used to emphasize the contrast with the negation. There isn't an exact English translation for **wel**, so note the emphasis in the examples:

A: **Wilt u suiker in de koffie?**
A: Would you like sugar in your coffee?

B: **Nee, maar** *wel* **melk, graag.**
B: No, but I *would* like milk, please.

A: **Heb je een auto?**
A: Do you have a car?

B: **Nee, maar ik heb** *wel* **twee fietsen.**
B: No, but I *do* have two bikes.

A: **Ik vind die film niet goed.**
A: I don't think that film is good.

B: **Ik vind die film** *wel* **goed.**
B: I *do* think it is good.

Exercise 15.1

Is the sentence correct or wrong, **goed** or **fout**?

1 Erik heeft niet tijd. goed – fout
2 Sanne gaat naar de yogales niet. goed – fout
3 Peter maakt geen huiswerk. goed – fout
4 Karin heeft geen goede tennisschoenen. goed – fout
5 Erik is thuis niet. goed – fout

Exercise 15.2

To negate the sentence, do you use **niet** or **geen**?

1 Karin is op school.   niet – geen
2 Ze heeft vandaag biologie.   niet – geen
3 Ze praat met haar lerares Duits.   niet – geen
4 Ze vindt Duits leuk.   niet – geen
5 In de pauze eet ze een kop soep.   niet – geen

Exercise 15.3

Fill in the blanks: **niet** or **geen**.

Situation: Erik is at a language school to sign up for lessons in French. The receptionist has lost or mixed up Erik's registration form with someone else's.

Receptionist: Is uw achternaam Van Buren?
Erik: Nee, mijn achternaam is _____ (1) Van Buren!
Receptionist: Zoekt u een cursus Arabisch?
Erik: Nee, ik zoek _____ (2) cursus Arabisch!
Receptionist: Woont u in Leeuwarden?
Erik: Nee, ik woon _____ (3) in Leeuwarden!
Receptionist: Heeft u mobiele telefoon?
Erik: Nee, ik heb _____ (4) mobiele telefoon!
Receptionist: Is dit uw emailadres?
Erik: Nee, dat is mijn emailadres _____ (5)!
Receptionist: Wilt u een nieuw formulier invullen?
Erik: Nee dank u, ik wil _____ (6) nieuw formulier invullen.

Exercise 15.4

Put a checkmark in the position of **niet** in order to make the sentence negative.

Example: Erik ___ gaat ___ vandaag ✓ naar ___ het taleninstituut ___.

1 Erik ___ praat ___ met de receptionist ___.
2 De receptionist ___ heeft ___ het formulier van Erik ___.
3 De cursus Frans ___ is ___ voor beginners ___.
4 De cursus Frans ___ is ___ op maandag en woensdag ___.
5 Erik ___ kan ___ de cursus Frans ___ dit semester ___ doen ___.
6 Erik ___ doet ___ de cursus ___ dit semester ___, maar ___ volgend semester ___.
7 De boeken voor de cursus ___ zijn ___ duur ___.
8 Erik ___ betaalt ___ het lesgeld ___ met creditcard ___.

Exercise 15.5

Make the sentences negative.

Situation: Sanne is at the market. Or is she?

1 Sanne is op de markt.

2 Zij heeft aardappels nodig.

3 Er zijn nieuwe aardappels.

4 De aardappels zijn duur.

5 Ze koopt deze week veel aardappels.

Exercise 15.6

Put the sentence parts in the correct order. Use the words in bold first.

1 in een restaurant – zijn – niet – Erik en Sanne – **vandaag**

2 mensen – niet – **er** – in het restaurant – veel – zitten

3 snel – brengt – de menukaart – **de ober** – niet

4 de soep van de dag – niet – **Erik** – neemt

5 bestellen – ook – **Sanne** – de soep van de dag – wil – niet

Exercise 15.7

Give a negative answer to the questions, using **niet** or **geen**. Use the correct *pronouns* when necessary.

Situation: Peter and Karin's cousins Sem and Sam are visiting. Erik is folding a load of laundry and doesn't know what belongs to whom. He asks:

1 Karin, is dit jouw rok?
   Karin: Nee, _____
2 Peter, heb jij een blauwe onderbroek?
   Peter: Nee pap, _____

3 Sanne, is deze spijkerbroek van Sem?
Sanne: Nee Erik, _____
4 Sem en Sam, zijn dit jullie handdoeken?
Sem and Sam: Nee oom Erik, _____
5 Sam, zijn deze tennissokken van jou?
Sam: Nee, _____

Exercise 15.8

Answer the questions using **nog** with **niet** or **geen** to contrast **al**.

Situation: It is 6.00 am. Sanne is up. Erik enters the kitchen. Nothing has happened (or been done) yet.

Erik	Sanne
1 Is er al koffie?	Nee, _____
2 Is de krant er al?	Nee, _____
3 Zijn de kinderen al wakker?	Nee, _____
4 Is de hond al uitgelaten?	Nee, _____
5 Is er al post?	Nee, _____

Exercise 15.9

Answer the questions using **meer** with **niet** or **geen** to contrast **nog**.

Situation: In the restaurant at Erik's workplace.

Customers	Person behind counter
1 Is er nog soep?	Nee, _____
2 Heeft u nog kroketten?	Nee, _____
3 Is die koffie nog warm?	Nee, _____
4 Is de keuken nog open?	Nee, _____
5 Is de chef er nog?	Nee, _____

Exercise 15.10

Answer the questions using **niet** or **geen** and **wel**, and follow the example.

Example: Wilt u melk in de thee? (citroen) *Nee, ik wil **geen** melk, maar ik wil **wel** citroen.*

1 Wil je een glas spa? (appelsap)

_____

2 Ga ja vanavond naar de film? (de disco)

_____

3 Wilt u peper op de biefstuk? (extra champignons)

_____

4 Wil je dit jaar naar Engeland op vakantie? (Frankrijk)

_____

5 Vind je Brad Pitt een goed acteur? (George Clooney)

_____

UNIT SIXTEEN
The diminutive

Introduction

While English uses adjectives such as 'small', 'little', 'tiny' to indicate that something is small, the Dutch use diminutive endings on nouns, even on proper names (English would add -y or -ie, as in Johnny, Ronnie, etc.). The diminutive is not only used to indicate that something is literally small in size, but it is also used to express different attitudes: positive or negative, endearment or contempt. We like our **kopje koffie**, our **glaasje wijn**, our **biertje**, our **koekje** and our **broodje kaas**. Some words exist only in the diminutive form: **meisje** 'girl', **sprookje** 'fairy tale', **toetje** 'dessert'. Children's games and proverbs often use diminutives: **touwtje springen** 'rope jumping'/'skipping', **vadertje en moedertje spelen** 'play mom and dad', **belletje trekken** 'ring someone's doorbell and run away'. The proverbial **huisje, boompje, beestje, Jantje, Pietje, Keesje** is the equivalent of the (American) English expression 'a house, a dog and a mini-van'. In short, the diminutive is as much a state of mind as it is a grammatical ending.

Examples

Sanne tells Erik about a shopping trip with her friend Lydia.

> **Gisteren ging ik met Lydia de stad in om een *kadootje* te kopen voor de nieuwe baby van Harry en Babette. We kochten een *knuffelbeestje* en een gebloemd *dekentje* voor de kinderwagen. Daarna gingen we een *kopje* koffie drinken. Er was nog één *tafeltje* vrij op het *terrasje* bij Van Doorn. Hm, het is pas maart, maar we konden toch al in het *zonnetje* zitten. Lydia gaat in april een *weekje* naar Kreta. Ze zei dat ze voor die tijd nog een paar *pondjes* wil afvallen, maar ze bestelde toch een *abrikozenschuitje* bij d'r koffie, haha!**
> Yesterday, I went to town with Lydia to buy a little gift for Harry and Babette's new baby. We bought a cuddly toy and a small blanket

with a flower design for the pram. After that, we went for a cup of
coffee. There was one free table left on the terrace at Van Doorn's.
Hm, it's only March, but we could already sit outside in the sun. Lydia
is going to Crete for a week in April. She said that she wants to shed
a few pounds before then, but she did order an apricot boat with her
coffee, haha!

Note the different endings on the diminutives: **kado*otje***, **knuffel-
beest*je***, **deken*tje***, **kop*je***, **tafel*tje***, **terras*je***, **zon*netje***, **week*je***, **pond*jes***,
abrikozenschuit*je*.

Diminutive endings: an overview

1 The most commonly used diminutive ending is **-je** at the end of a noun:
het huis – het huisje 'house', **de klok – het klokje** 'clock', **de brief – het
briefje** 'letter', **het boek – het boekje** 'book', **het bord – het bordje** 'plate',
'sign', **de tas – het tasje** 'bag'. The diminutive article is always **het**, all
diminutives are **het**-words. When the last letters of a word make it difficult
to pronounce it with the ending **-je**, other endings appear.
2 The second most commonly used ending is **-tje**. It is added firstly
to nouns ending in a vowel. Nouns ending in **-a**, **-o**, **-u**, and **-é** double
the vowel: **laatje** 'drawer', **autootje**, **parapluutje** 'umbrella', **cafeetje**.
Secondly, it is added to nouns with a long vowel ending in **-n**, **-l**, **-r**:
boontje 'bean', **schaaltje** 'bowl', **deurtje** 'door'. Thirdly, it is added to
nouns ending in unstressed **-er**, **-el**, **-en**, **-or**: **kamertje**, **lepeltje** 'spoon',
keukentje 'kitchen', **professortje**. And lastly, it is added to nouns ending in **-w**: **vrouwtje** 'little woman', **duwtje** 'push'. See 1–4 in the table.
3 The third diminutive ending is **-etje**. It is added to nouns ending in **-l**,
-m, **-n**, **-ng**, and **-r** preceded by a short, stressed vowel. Many of the mono-
syllabic words such as **man**, **bal** *'ball'*, **bon** 'receipt', 'ticket', **ring**, and
kar 'cart', 'waggon' fall under this category: **mannetje**, **balletje**, **bonnetje**,
ringetje, **karretje**. Examples of words with more than one syllable are:
ballonnetje, **kartonnetje**, **vriendinnetje** 'girl friend'. Some nouns ending
in **-b**, **-p**, and **-g** also belong in this group: **krabbetje** 'crab', **slabbetje** 'bib',
bruggetje 'bridge', **vlaggetje** 'flag', **weggetje** 'road', **kippetje** 'chicken',
poppetje 'doll'. Note the alternative forms: **brugje**, **kipje**, **popje**. See
5–6 in the table.
4 The ending **-pje** is added to nouns ending in **-m** preceded by a long vowel:
raampje 'window', **bloempje**, (also: **bloemetje**) 'flower', **boompje** 'tree',
zeempje 'shammy'. Secondly, it is added to nouns ending in the letters
-lm or **-rm**: **filmpje**, **wormpje**. Thirdly, nouns ending in unstressed **-um**
or **-em** also have this diminutive ending: **museumpje**, **bezempje** 'broom'.
See 7, 8 and 9 in the table.

5 The ending **-kje** is added to some, but not all nouns ending in **-ing**; the diminutive, for example, of **koning** 'king' is **koninkje**, and of **woning** 'apartment', 'dwelling' is **woninkje**. Note that the **-g** of **-ing** is dropped. But many words ending in **-ing** have the ending **-etje**: **tekeningetje** 'drawing', **leerlingetje** 'pupil'. See 10 in the table.

Some diminutives are irregular. See 11 in the table.

Diminutive endings other than **-je**

-tje	-etje	-pje	-kje
a ⇒ aatje 1 o ⇒ ootje u ⇒ uutje é ⇒ eetje (étje) i(e) ⇒ ietje	short vowel + 5 -l ⇒ lletje -m ⇒ mmetje -n ⇒ nnetje -ng ⇒ ngetje -r ⇒ rretje	long vowel + 7 -m ⇒ pje	unstressed 10 -ing ⇒ inkje however: *leerlingetje* *tekeningetje*
long vowel + 2 -n ⇒ ntje -l ⇒ ltje -r ⇒ rtje		-lm ⇒ lmpje 8 -rm ⇒ rmpje	irregulars 11 blad – blaadje gat – gaatje glas – glaasje
unstressed 3 -er ⇒ ertje -el ⇒ eltje -en ⇒ entje -or ⇒ ortje	-b ⇒ bbetje 6 -g ⇒ ggetje -p ⇒ ppetje also: *brugje, popje*	unstressed 9 -em ⇒ empje -um ⇒ umpje	lot – lootje pad – paadje schip – scheepje staf – staafje rad – raadje
-w ⇒ wtje 4			vat – vaatje

Exercise 16.1

Here are some titles of well-known Dutch children's songs. Underline the diminutives and for each underlined noun, find the ground word in the singular.

Example: Drie kleine <u>kleutertjes</u>. *kleuter*

1 Donzen gele kuikentjes. _____
2 Er zat een aapje op een stokje. _____
3 Hoedje van papier. _____
4 Hop paardje hop. _____
5 Op een klein stationnetje. _____
6 Parapluutje, parasolletje. _____
7 Rije, rije rije in een wagentje. _____
8 Twee emmertjes water halen. _____

9 Wij maken een kringetje.   _____

10 Zakdoekje leggen.   _____

Exercise 16.2

For each item, find the matching noun, and put it in the diminutive: **glas,
beker, bord, lepel, schaal, kop, plak, schijf, fles, stuk.**

Situation: What Erik likes to eat and drink and when.

1 Bij het ontbijt drinkt Erik een _____ koffie.
2 Hij doet een _____ suiker in de koffie.
3 Bij de lunch neemt hij een boterham met twee _____ kaas.
4 Hij drinkt bij de lunch een _____ water.
5 Hij doet een _____ citroen in het water.
6 Na de lunch eet hij een _____ Yoplait vruchtenyoghurt.
7 's Middags bij de thee eet hij het liefst een _____ appeltaart.
8 Bij het avondeten houdt hij van een lekker _____ soep.
9 Bij een voetbalwedstrijd drinkt hij altijd een _____ bier.
10 En 's avonds bij de televisie? Een heerlijk _____ pinda's, hmmm!

Exercise 16.3

Enter a noun in the diminutive form in each blank. The context (and the
first letter of the noun) will tell you which word you need.

*Situation: Karin is babysitting her neighbor's son, and she is making up
a bedside story.*

Meneer Liliput
Meneer Liliput woont in een heel klein h_____ (1). In de garage staat
een heel klein a_____ (2). Achter het huis ligt een piepklein
t_____ (3) met kleurige kleine b_____ (4). Meneer Liliput
slaapt in een heel klein b_____ (5). Elke morgen drinkt hij een
g_____ (6) melk en eet hij een b_____ (7) kaas. Meneer
Liliput gaat op een klein f_____ (8) naar zijn werk. Daar zit hij aan
een klein b_____ (9) op een klein s_____ (10) Hij maakt notities op een klein p_____ (11). Om vijf uur komt meneer Liliput thuis.
Hij kookt soep in een klein p_____ (12) op zijn kleine f_____
(13) in zijn kleine k_____ (14). Daarna eet hij de soep in een klein
b_____ (15). Terwijl hij de soep eet, kijkt hij naar zijn kleine
t_____ (16).

Exercise 16.4

Put the words between brackets into the diminutive form.

Situation: A story about Pluto, Erik's neighbor's dog.

1 De buurvrouw heeft een klein (hond) _____ met de naam Pluto.
2 Ze laat Pluto in het (tuin) _____ achter haar (woning) _____ spelen.
3 Soms gaat ze naar het (park) _____ bij het winkelcentrum.
4 Daar laat ze Pluto achter een (bal) _____ aan rennen.
5 Af en toe piest Pluto tegen een (boom) _____ .
6 Als het regent, draagt mijn buurvrouw een (paraplu) _____ .
7 En als het heel koud is, trekt ze Pluto een wollen (jas) _____ aan.
8 Pluto jaagt op de (eekhoorn) _____ .
9 Maar hij kan niet zo hard lopen, want zijn (poten) _____ zijn te kort.
10 De eekhoorn lacht en gooit (eikels) _____ op Pluto's kop.

Exercise 16.5

Put the nouns between brackets into the diminutive form.

Situation: Erik and Sanne are looking around in a department store. Sanne goes to buy a few things for her friend's new baby. Erik goes to the deli. When they meet at the exit, they talk about their purchases.

Erik: Hoi, wat heb je gekocht?
Sanne: O, het was heel moeilijk. Ze hadden zulke leuke (dingen) _____ (1). Ik zag een schattig wollen (jurk) _____ (2). maar dat was erg duur. En ze hadden geen (sokken) _____ (3) in roze, jammer. Ik heb nu een (trui) _____ (4) gekocht, alvast voor de winter, en een geblokt (deken) _____ (5), ook heel leuk, en ik ga nog een of ander leuk (speelgoed) _____ (6) zoeken. En jij?
Erik: O, ik heb voor vanavond een heerlijk (stuk) _____ (7) paté gevonden, daar heb ik thuis een lekker (wijn) _____ (8) bij, en ze hadden (noten) _____ (9) in de aanbieding, daar heb ik een (zak) _____ (10) van gekocht, en verder nog een (kilo) _____ (11) oude kaas.
Sanne: Zo veel? Dat krijg ik op de markt goedkoper!
Erik: Ach, zeur niet, we maken er een gezellig (avond) _____ (12) van, ja toch?

Exercise 16.6

The Dutch have a lot of colloquial usage of diminutive forms. Here are
some common idiomatic phrases. Can you find the right word for each one?
Choose from: **dutje, hapje, ommetje, biertje, praatje**.

Situation: Wat doen Erik en Sanne vanmiddag?

1 Sanne gaat even een _____ doen (take a nap).
2 Daarna gaat ze even een _____ maken (take a short walk).
3 Om zes uur gaan ze een _____ eten (have a bite to eat).
4 Erik gaat even een _____ maken met de buurman (have a chat).
5 Misschien wil de buurman wel even een _____ pakken (grab a beer).

UNIT SEVENTEEN
Separable and inseparable verbs

Introduction

This chapter discusses verbs with separable and those with inseparable prefixes. Intonation (stress) plays an important role in determining whether a verb is separable or inseparable. Most separable prefixes are stressed: **ópbellen** 'call', 'phone', **úitgaan** 'go out', **ínvullen** 'fill in', 'complete', **nádenken** 'think', 'ponder'. Most inseparable prefixes are unstressed: **bestéllen** 'order', **erváren** 'experience', **gelóven** 'believe', **herkénnen** 'recognize', **ontmóeten** 'meet', **vergéten** 'forget'. Note: the accents indicate emphasis.

Separable verbs

What is going on in the Beumer family today? Examples of separable verbs:

Sanne *belt* **opa en oma Beumer** *op.*	Sanne calls grandpa and grandma Beumer.
Erik *vult* **een belastingformulier** *in.*	Erik is completing a tax form.
Peter *maakt* **zijn voetbalschoenen** *schoon.*	Peter is cleaning his soccer shoes.
Karin *gaat* **met een vriendin** *uit.*	Karin is going out with a friend.
Sanne <u>moet</u> **de ontbijtborden** *afwassen.*	Sanne has to wash the breakfast dishes.
Erik <u>wil</u> **vandaag lekker** *thuisblijven.*	Erik wants to stay in today.

The separable part of the verb is often a preposition or an adverb. In most cases, the original meaning of the preposition or adverb is still obvious in combination with the main verb, for example *op*staan 'stand up', 'get up' and *schoon*maken 'clean'. In other cases it is less obvious: *aan*steken 'light a fire', *uit*leggen 'explain'. And sometimes, the separable part has no meaning of its own: *teleur*stellen 'disappoint'.

Some
frequently
used
prefixes
that are
always
separated

Some frequently used prefixes that are always separated

af-	**afwassen**	do dishes	**afhalen**	pick up
bij-	**bijstellen**	adjust	**bijhouden**	keep up
mee-	**meegaan**	go with	**meenemen**	take with
na-	**nadenken**	ponder	**nakijken**	check, examine
neer-	**neerleggen**	lay down	**neerslaan**	knock down
op-	**opstaan**	get up	**opbellen**	call, phone
rond-	**rondkijken**	look around	**rondrennen**	run around
tegen-	**tegenkomen**	run into, meet	**tegenspreken**	contradict
terug-	**terugbellen**	call back	**teruggaan**	return
uit	**uitnodigen**	invite	**uitspreken**	pronounce

In a main clause (sentence), the separable part of the verb goes to the very end:

Erik *denkt* **over een probleem** *na.*	Erik thinks deeply about a problem.
Hoe *spreek* **je dit woord** *uit?*	How do you pronounce this word?
Sanne *nodigt* **een vriendin** *uit.*	Sanne invites a friend.

However, when there is a modal verb (**kunnen, laten, moeten, mogen, willen, zullen**) in the sentence, the modal verb (the conjugated verb) takes the second position, and the separable verb (infinitive) goes to the end of the sentence.

Erik *moet* **over een probleem** *nadenken.*	Erik has to think deeply about a problem.
Sanne *wil* **een vriendin** *uitnodigen.*	Sanne wants to invite a friend.

Some prefixes that are not always separated

Some prefixes are not always separated from the main verb. To determine whether the verb will split or not, one has to know the pronunciation of the verb, i.e. where the emphasis lies. In the table below, the emphasis is indicated with accents.

Separable			Inseparable	
aan-	**áánkomen**	arrive	**aanbídden**	worship
door-	**dóórgaan**	go on	**doorstáán**	endure
mis-	**mísgaan**	fail	**mislúkken**	fail
om-	**ómleiden**	divert	**omgéven**	surround
onder-	**ónderbrengen**	house, lodge	**ondernémen**	undertake
over-	**óversteken**	cross street	**overléggen**	negotiate
voor-	**vóórkomen**	happen, occur	**voorkómen**	prevent
weer-	**wéérgeven**	summarize	**weerstáán**	resist

As you can see in the table, sometimes a verb has two forms: separable and inseparable. They differ in meaning. Example:

Als we het *voorkómen*, *komt* het niet meer *vóór*.
If we prevent it, it won't happen again.

Prefixes that are always inseparable

be-	**bestellen**	order	**bewaren**	keep, save
er-	**ervaren**	experience	**erkennen**	accede, admit
ge-	**geloven**	believe	**gedenken**	commemorate
her-	**herhalen**	repeat	**herinneren**	remember
ont-	**ontdekken**	discover	**ontmoeten**	meet
ver-	**vergeten**	forget	**vertrouwen**	trust

Erik *vergeet* zijn sleutels.	Erik forgets his keys.
Sanne *ontdekt* een leuk nieuw restaurant.	Sanne discovers a nice new restaurant.
Karin *bewaart* haar ringen in een doosje.	Karin keeps her rings in a small box.
Peter *bestelt* een pizza margharita.	Peter orders a pizza margharita.

Note: Sometimes, inseparable prefixes carry a certain meaning or function. The prefix **be-**, for instance, changes an intransitive verb with a preposition into a transitive verb, for example **kijken naar** into **bekijken**, sometimes giving the action described a more intensive meaning. The prefix **ver-** often signals a change in state or condition, for example in verbs such as **veranderen** 'change', **verdikken** 'thicken', **versmelten** 'melt together'. The prefix **her-** indicates that something is done again. The verb **herhalen** 'repeat' is by far the best example, but others such as **herschrijven** 'rewrite' and **herdenken** 'remember', 'commemorate' are also good examples. Lastly, the prefix **ont-** indicates that something is being undone, as in

ontdekken 'discover', literally 'uncover', **ontgroeien** 'grow out of', **ontharen** 'shave', literally 'remove hair'.

Note the change of an intransitive verb with a preposition to a transitive verb with **be-**.

Erik kijkt naar een foto ⇒ **Erik** *bekijkt* **een foto.**
Erik looks at a photograph.

Sanne antwoordt op een email ⇒ **Sanne** *beantwoordt* **een email.**
Sanne answers an email.

De klas spreekt over een thema ⇒ **De klas** *bespreekt* **een thema.**
The class discusses a topic.

We klimmen op de berg ⇒ **We** *beklimmen* **de berg.**
We climb the mountain.

Inseparable verbs with **be-** can also be derived from transitive verbs, as in **water gieten** 'pour water' versus **de planten begieten** 'water the plants', or **een essay schrijven** 'write an essay' versus **een situatie beschrijven** 'describe a situation'. Some are derived from nouns, as in **bestraten** 'pave' from **straat** 'street' or **bespiegelen** 'reflect on' from **spiegel** 'mirror'. Lastly, adjectives can form verbs with **be-** such as **bezuinigen** 'save', 'economize' from **zuinig** 'thrifty' or **bevuilen** 'soil' from **vuil** 'dirty'.

Adverbs and nouns as separable prefixes

In the dictionary, separable and inseparable verbs are listed by their prefixes. Many adverbs and nouns can function as a separable prefix. Some examples:

open-	**opendoen**	open	**opensnijden**	cut open
samen-	**samenwonen**	live together	**samenstellen**	compile
thuis-	**thuisblijven**	stay home	**thuiskomen**	come home
vast-	**vasthouden**	hold on to	**vaststaan**	stand firm
weg-	**wegbrengen**	take away	**weggooien**	discard

Some examples of nouns as prefixes are *de adem* ⇒ **ademhalen** 'breathe', *de auto* ⇒ **autorijden** 'drive', *de les* ⇒ **lesgeven** 'teach' and *de plaats* ⇒ **plaatsvinden** 'take place'.

There is more information on separable and inseparable verbs in Units 19, 22 and 23 and in *Intermediate Dutch*. For the present perfect of separable and inseparable verbs, see Unit 18.

Exercise 17.1

In Peter's answers, take the modal verb out and separate the verb.

Erik	Peter
1 Je moet je kamer opruimen.	Ja, ik _____ nu mijn kamer _____.
2 Je moet oma opbellen.	Okee, _____.
3 Je moet de pizza ophalen.	Goed, _____.
4 Je moet je jas aantrekken.	Jaha, _____.
5 Je moet je huiswerk afmaken.	Nee, _____!
6 Je moet vanavond thuisblijven.	Nee, _____!

Exercise 17.2

Separate the separable verbs from the inseparable verbs: **aankomen, afspreken, bespreken, uitgeven, instappen, geloven, aankleden, uittrekken, vertrekken, ontwerpen, doorwerken, herkennen, meewerken, bewerken, verfilmen, langskomen, thuisblijven, tegenwerken, aanbieden, verbieden, opnemen, ontnemen.**

Separable: _____

_____

_____

_____

Inseparable: _____

_____

_____

_____

Exercise 17.3

Put the matching parts together to form new separable verbs. You may need a dictionary.

stil-	-brengen	1	to stop
hard-	-keuren	2	to run
goed-	-staan	3	to approve
kwijt-	-lopen	4	to lose
groot-	-raken	5	to raise

Exercise 17.4

Read the information in Unit 18 on separable and inseparable verbs in the present perfect, and then proceed to do this exercise. Put the sentences into the present perfect tense.

Situation: What did Erik and his family do today?

1 Erik (een zakenvriend ontmoeten) _____
2 Sanne (oma Beumer opbellen) _____
3 Peter (met een vriend uitgaan) _____
4 Karin (lang uitslapen) _____
5 Erik (zijn paraplu vergeten) _____
6 Sanne (de meubels afstoffen) _____
7 Karin (met een breiwerk beginnen) _____
8 Peter (de vriend voor het eten uitnodigen) _____

UNIT EIGHTEEN
The present perfect tense

Introduction

The present perfect tense in English, for example 'I have worked', is much more linked to the present than the Dutch present perfect **Ik heb gewerkt**. When speakers of English talk about past events, they prefer to use the simple past tense: 'I worked'. They use the present perfect to express events that last into the present such as 'I have lived here for three years' (that is, I am still living here) or 'I have seen that film six times' (and I may see it again). The Dutch commonly use the simple past (**Ik werkte**) for the narration of repeated events in the past (things one used to do, for instance) or for a series of events in the past. Consequently, the simple past is used more in written Dutch, and the present perfect is used more in spoken Dutch. The present perfect is used for the narration of completed, non-recurrent events in the past, often accompanied by words such as **gisteren**, **een maand geleden**, **vorige week**, etc.

Examples

> **Sanne *is* gisteren naar de markt *geweest*.**
> Sanne went to the market yesterday.

> **Erik *heeft* vorige week een nieuwe auto *gekocht*.**
> Erik bought a new car last week.

> **Peter *heeft* een maand geleden examen *gedaan*.**
> Peter did his exams a month ago.

> **Karin *heeft* een week bij oma *gelogeerd*.**
> Karin stayed with grandma for a week.

As one can see in the examples, the present perfect tense in Dutch consists of an auxiliary verb, **hebben** or **zijn**, and a past participle. In a main clause, the auxiliary (the conjugated verb) takes the second position, and the past participle is placed at the end of the sentence. Dutch differs from English here; in English the auxiliary and the participle stay closer together.

The present perfect of regular (weak) verbs

Examples in context. What did the Beumers do yesterday?

Erik *heeft* **de hele dag in de tuin** *gewerkt.*	Erik worked in the garden all day.
Sanne *heeft* **met Ina tennis** *gespeeld.*	Sanne played tennis with Ina.
Peter *heeft* **met Johan huiswerk** *gemaakt.*	Peter did homework with Johan.
Karin *heeft* **met oma** *getelefoneerd.*	Karin talked to grandma on the phone.

The past participle of a regular (weak) verb begins with **ge-** and ends in **-t** or **-d**. Past participles of verbs with a stem ending in **-p**, **-t**, **-k**, **-f**, **-s** and **-ch** end in **-t**, and those of verbs with a stem ending in a soft consonant such as **-m**, **-n**, **-l**, **-r**, **-b**, **-d**, **-g**, **-v**, **-w** and **-z** end in **-d**. An easy way to remember the past participles ending in **-t** is to make a word with the hard consonants: 'T FoKSCHaaP, 'the breeding sheep'.

A few words on **spelling**. The past participle of a verb with an open syllable doubles the vowel: **ma-ken** ⇒ **gem*aa*kt**, **spe-len** ⇒ **gesp*ee*ld**. Past participles of regular verbs with a stem ending in **-v** or **-z** end in **-d**, even though the **-d** is preceded by **-f** or **-s**: **leven** 'live' ⇒ *geleefd*, **reizen** 'travel' ⇒ *gereisd*. Lastly, weak verbs with double consonants in the stem drop one in the past participle: **zetten** 'put' ⇒ **heeft gezet**, **wedden** 'bet' ⇒ **heeft gewed**, **zakken** 'drop', 'fail' ⇒ **is gezakt**, **boffen** 'be lucky' ⇒ **heeft geboft**, **passen** 'fit' ⇒ **heeft gepast**.

The present perfect of strong verbs

Examples in context:

Peter *heeft* **veel televisie** *gekeken.*	Peter watched TV a lot.
Hij *heeft* **twee boeken** *gelezen.*	He read two books.
Karin *heeft* **met Cindy koffie** *gedronken.*	Karin had coffee with Cindy.
Ze *heeft* **Annie in huis** *geholpen.*	She helped Annie in the house.

The past participle of a strong verb begins with **ge-** and ends in **-en**, and in many cases the *stem vowel changes*. The most frequent vowel changes are:

113

$ij \Rightarrow e$	**kijken** $\Rightarrow$ **gekeken, snijden** $\Rightarrow$ **gesneden, blijven** $\Rightarrow$ **gebleven**
$i \Rightarrow e$	**liggen** $\Rightarrow$ **gelegen, bidden** $\Rightarrow$ **gebeden, zitten** $\Rightarrow$ **gezeten**
$i \Rightarrow o$	**drinken** $\Rightarrow$ **gedronken, zingen** $\Rightarrow$ **gezongen, beginnen** $\Rightarrow$ **begonnen**
$ie \Rightarrow o$	**vliegen** $\Rightarrow$ **gevlogen, kiezen** $\Rightarrow$ **gekozen, schieten** $\Rightarrow$ **geschoten**
$ui \Rightarrow o$	**ruiken** $\Rightarrow$ **geroken, buigen** $\Rightarrow$ **gebogen, schuiven** $\Rightarrow$ **geschoven**
$e \Rightarrow o$	**nemen** $\Rightarrow$ **genomen, zwemmen** $\Rightarrow$ **gezwommen, helpen** $\Rightarrow$ **geholpen**

For more examples, check the Appendix in the back of this book.

When to use hebben and when to use zijn

Most of the time, we use the auxiliary **hebben** in the present perfect tense. Only verbs that express motion *with a clear indication of going somewhere* (**fietsen** 'bike', **rijden** 'drive', **lopen** 'walk', **gaan** 'go', **vliegen** 'fly', **reizen** 'travel', **rennen** 'run', **varen** 'sail') and verbs that express a *change of condition or substance* (**smelten** 'melt', **veranderen** 'change', **worden** 'become') take **zijn** in the present perfect. Examples:

Erik *is* naar de supermarkt *gegaan*.	Erik went to the supermarket.
Hij *heeft* vanille-ijs *gekocht*.	He bought vanilla ice-cream.
Hij *is* met het ijs naar huis *gefietst*.	He rode home with the ice-cream.
Thuis *heeft* hij de tas *uitgepakt*.	He unpacked his bag at home.
En ja hoor, het ijs *is* *gesmolten*.	And lo, the ice-cream had melted.

Some verbs, however, take **zijn** even though they don't necessarily express motion or change: **beginnen** 'begin', **stoppen** 'stop', **ophouden** 'stop', 'quit', **blijven** 'stay', **komen** 'come', **gebeuren** 'happen'.

The present perfect of hebben and zijn

The present perfect of **hebben** is *heeft gehad* and of **zijn** it is *is geweest*.

Sanne *heeft* een leuke dag *gehad*.	Sanne has had a nice day.
Ze *is* met Karin naar de stad *geweest*.	She went to town (was in town) with Karin.

For these two verbs, however, we often prefer to use the simple past: 'had', 'was'.

Sanne *had* een leuke dag.
Ze *was* met Karin naar de stad.

The present perfect of separable verbs

The participle of a separable verb is formed by putting **-ge-** in between the prefix and the rest of the verb. Examples:

Erik heeft het huis schoon*ge*maakt.	Erik cleaned the house.
Hij heeft de kamers op*ge*ruimd.	He tidied up the rooms.
Hij heeft overal stof af*ge*nomen.	He dusted everywhere.
Sanne heeft tuinboontjes in*ge*vroren.	Sanne froze garden peas.

Otherwise, all other rules for the formation of strong or weak past participles apply.

The present perfect of inseparable verbs

Verbs with unstressed prefixes such as **be-, er-, ge-, her-, ont-** and **ver-** *do not* form their past participles with **ge-**. Otherwise, all other rules for the formation of strong or weak past participles apply. Examples:

Erik heeft de gasrekening niet *be*taald.	Erik didn't pay the gas bill.
Hij heeft het deze maand *ver*geten.	He forgot this month.
Hij heeft het te laat *ont*dekt.	He discovered it too late.
Sanne heeft het niet *ge*loofd!	Sanne didn't believe it!

Note: the verb **vergeten** can appear with **hebben** or **zijn**. In the sentence **Ik *heb* mijn tas vergeten**, simple negligence is meant, just forgetting a physical object, whereas in the sentence **Ik *ben* zijn telefoonnummer vergeten**, the speaker no longer has that information. In speech, however, this distinction is often neglected.

Some irregular forms

Some verbs don't seem to follow either the rules for weak verbs or the rules for strong verbs or have other irregularities: **brengen** 'bring' ⇒ **heeft gebracht, denken** 'think' ⇒ **heeft gedacht, doen** 'do' ⇒ **heeft gedaan, eten** 'eat' ⇒ **heeft gegeten, gaan** 'go' ⇒ **is gegaan, kopen** 'buy' ⇒ **heeft gekocht, slaan** 'hit' ⇒ **heeft geslagen, staan** 'stand' ⇒ **heeft gestaan, zien** 'see' ⇒ **heeft gezien, zoeken** 'look for' ⇒ **heeft gezocht.** It is best to keep a list of irregular and mixed verbs and their vowel changes as you acquire new vocabulary.

The present perfect of sentences with modal verbs

Sentences with modal verbs form the present perfect with the auxiliary **hebben**. Neither the modal verb nor the main verb turns into a past participle. Instead, they both move to the end of the sentence and stay in their infinitive form. The infinitive of the main verb always follows the infinitive of the modal auxiliary.

Erik *heeft* de rekening *moeten betalen.* Erik had to pay the bill.
Maar hij *heeft* het niet *kunnen doen.* But he couldn't do it.

Only modal auxiliaries that can be used independently have a past participle: **kunnen-gekund, moeten-gemoeten, willen-gewild, mogen-gemogen.** Example:

Ik heb dat niet *gewild.* I didn't want that.

Exercise 18.1

For each weak verb, decide whether the past participle ends in **-d** or **-t.**

1 bewaren 'keep', 'save' d
2 delen 'share'
3 fietsen 'bike'
4 halen 'fetch'
5 horen 'hear'
6 koken 'cook', 'boil'
7 leren 'learn'
8 pakken 'grab', 'pack'
9 passen 'fit'
10 redden 'save'
11 ruilen 'exchange'
12 vragen 'ask'
13 wachten 'wait'
14 wandelen 'hike', 'walk'
15 werken 'work'

Exercise 18.2

Enter **heb** or **ben.**

Situation: Wendy is telling Sanne about her vacation in New York.

Ik _____ (1) het Vrijheidsbeeld (statue of liberty) gezien. Ik _____ (2) in Chinatown heel lekker gegeten. Ik _____ (3) naar een Broadwayshow gegaan. Ik _____ (4) met aardige Amerikanen gepraat. Ik _____ (5) bij Saks Fifth Avenue geweest. Ik _____ (6) daar een heel dure blouse gekocht. Ik _____ (7) heel weinig geslapen! Ik _____ (8) twee kilo dikker geworden! Ik _____ (9) een zalige vakantie gehad. Ik _____ (10) gisteren thuisgekomen.

Exercise 18.3

Enter a form of **hebben** or **zijn**.

Situation: Sanne talks to her nosy neighbor, who wants to know who was visiting yesterday.

1 Buurvrouw: Wie _____ je gisteren op bezoek gehad?
2 Sanne: O, Alex en Ina _____ bij ons op bezoek geweest.
3 Buurvrouw: Leuk, en wat _____ jullie gedaan?
4 Sanne: We _____ een stukje de stad in gewandeld en we _____ op een terrasje koffie gedronken.
5 Buurvrouw: En hoe laat _____ Alex en Ina weer weggegaan?
6 Sanne: Ongeveer om tien uur _____ ze de trein genomen. We _____ ze naar het station gebracht. En jullie?
7 Buurvrouw: Wij _____ maar thuisgebleven. Piet _____ naar het voetbal gekeken. De hele dag die tv aan, bah!

Exercise 18.4

Fill in the past participle. Follow the vowel change model. The Dutch word for past participle is **voltooid deelwoord**.

1 Het deelwoord van <u>gieten</u> is *gegoten* en dat van <u>schieten</u> is _____.
2 Het deelwoord van <u>stijgen</u> is *gestegen* en dat van <u>krijgen</u> is _____.
3 Het deelwoord van <u>drinken</u> is *gedronken* en dat van <u>stinken</u> is _____.
4 Het deelwoord van <u>fluiten</u> is *gefloten* en dat van <u>sluiten</u> is _____.
5 Het deelwoord van <u>breken</u> is *gebroken* en dat van <u>spreken</u> is _____.

Exercise 18.5

Fill in the correct form of the past participle. A star (*) indicates that the verb is strong.

Situation: Peter and Johan talk about what they did last night.

Peter: Wat heb jij gisteren (doen*) _____ (1)?
Johan: O, niet veel. Ik heb eerst naar een nieuwe cd (luisteren) _____ (2) en later een beetje voor het proefwerk biologie (leren) _____ (3). Ik heb even met Lies (mailen) _____ (4) en tv (kijken*) _____ (5). Heb je die voetbalwedstrijd nog (zien*) _____ (6)?
Peter: Nee, ik ben met m'n vader naar een tennistoernooi (zijn) _____ (7).

Johan: Hé, heb jij die taak voor wiskunde al (maken) _____ (8)?

Peter: Ja, dit zijn mijn antwoorden. Heb jij dat hoofdstuk geschiedenis (lezen*) _____ (9)? Waar gaat dat over?

Johan: Eh, over hoe de tweede wereldoorlog (beginnen*) _____ (10) is.

Exercise 18.6

Rewrite the sentences in the present perfect.

Situation: Buying a new dress.

1 Linda gaat met de tram naar het centrum.

2 Ze zoekt bij de Bijenkorf een nieuwe jurk uit.

3 Ze trekt de jurk in de paskamer aan.

4 Ze betaalt de jurk met creditcard.

5 Een dag later brengt ze de jurk terug.

UNIT NINETEEN
The simple past tense

Introduction

As mentioned in the previous chapter, in Dutch the simple past tense (also called the imperfect) is used for the narration of 1 recurrent events or 2 a series of events in the past. Examples:

1 **We *gingen* vroeger vaak naar opa en oma. Opa *speelde* spelletjes met ons, hij *ging* met ons wandelen en hij *maakte* graag muziek met ons. Oma *kookte* de beste havermout voor het ontbijt en we *kregen* 's morgens voor het opstaan een koekje op bed.**
We went (used to go) to grandpa and grandma a lot. Grandpa played games with us, he went for walks with us and he liked to play music with us. Grandma cooked the best oatmeal for breakfast and each morning before getting up we would get a cookie.

2 **Ik *kwam* gisteren laat thuis. Ik *nam* een biertje uit de koelkast, *deed* de televisie aan en *keek* nog even naar het laatste nieuws. Toen *ging* ik naar bed.**
I came home late last night. I took a beer from the fridge, turned the TV on and watched the late news. Then I went to bed.

Note the difference between the regular (weak) and the strong verbs (see words in italic). The forms **speelde**, **kookte** and **maakte** are regular, and all of the italic forms in 2 are strong verbs.

The simple past tense of regular verbs

The simple past tense of regular (weak) verbs is formed by adding the ending -te to verb stems ending in one of the consonants of 'T FoKSCHaaP (**p, t, k, f, s, ch**). There are only two forms: singular and plural ⇒ **maakte**, **maakten**. The conjugation of the simple past of **maken** is therefore as follows: **ik maakte, jij maakte, u maakte, hij/zij/het maakte, wij maakten, jullie maakten, zij maakten**. Examples:

Peter *maakte* met Johan huiswerk.	Peter did homework with Johan.
Sanne *kookte* soep voor zondag.	Sanne cooked soup for Sunday.

The ending **-de** is added to verb stems ending in a soft consonant. The conjugation of the simple past of **spelen** is therefore as follows: **ik speelde, jij speelde, u speelde, hij/zij/het speelde, wij speelden, jullie speelden, zij speelden**. Examples:

Erik *speelde* gisteren tennis.	Erik played tennis yesterday.
Karin *telefoneerde* met een vriendin.	Karin spoke with a friend on the phone.

A few notes on spelling. Verbs with a long single vowel and an open syllable such as **maken, koken, spelen**, etc. double the vowel in the simple past: **maakte, kookte, speelde**. The letters **-z-** or **-v-** in the stem of verbs such as **reizen** and **leven** become voiceless before the ending **-de**: **reisde, leefde**. Verbs with single or double **-t-** or **-d-** in the stem such as **zetten** 'put', **redden** 'rescue', **praten** 'talk' and **antwoorden** 'answer' double the **-t-** or **-d-** in the simple past: **zette, redde, praatte, beantwoordde**. Other double consonants, however, are reduced to one: **zakken ⇒ zakte, passen ⇒ paste, krabben ⇒ krabde, leggen ⇒ legde**, and so on.

The simple past of strong verbs

The simple past of strong verbs always involves a vowel change. Examples:

Erik *ging* voor de lunch naar de kantine.
Erik went to the canteen for lunch.

Hij *nam* een broodje en een kop koffie.
He took a sandwich and a cup of coffee.

Hij *at* aan tafel bij een paar collega's.
He ate with a few colleagues at their table.

Maar hij *dronk* de koffie in z'n bureau.
But he drank the coffee in his office.

Many verbs follow the same vowel change pattern in the simple past. Examples:

ij ⇒ *ee*	**blijven** ⇒ **bleef, kijken** ⇒ **keek, snijden** ⇒ **sneed**
i ⇒ *a*	**bidden** ⇒ **bad, liggen** ⇒ **lag, zitten** ⇒ **zat**
i ⇒ *o*	**beginnen** ⇒ **begon, drinken** ⇒ **dronk, zingen** ⇒ **zong**
ie ⇒ *oo*	**kiezen** ⇒ **koos, schieten** ⇒ **schoot, vliegen** ⇒ **vloog**
ui ⇒ *oo*	**buigen** ⇒ **boog, ruiken** ⇒ **rook, schuiven** ⇒ **schoof**
e ⇒ *a*	**breken** ⇒ **brak, nemen** ⇒ **nam, stelen** ⇒ **stal**
e ⇒ *o*	**gelden** ⇒ **gold, trekken** ⇒ **trok, zwemmen** ⇒ **zwom**
a ⇒ *oe*	**dragen** ⇒ **droeg, graven** ⇒ **groef, varen** ⇒ **voer**
a ⇒ *ie*	**blazen** ⇒ **blies, laten** ⇒ **liet, slapen** ⇒ **sliep**

The simple past tense of separable verbs

Examples in context:

Erik *belde* **een klant** *op*.	Erik phoned a client.
Ze *spraken* **in de stad** *af*.	They agreed to meet in town.
Ze *namen* **een contract** *door*.	They went over a contract.
De klant *vulde* **een formulier** *in*.	The client filled in a form.

The simple past tense for separable verbs follows the rules for regular and irregular verbs. The main verb, in the simple past form, takes the second position in the sentence, and the separable prefix remains at the end of the sentence.

The simple past tense of inseparable verbs

Examples in context:

Erik *betaalde* **de gasrekening niet.**	Erik didn't pay the gas bill.
Hij *vergat* **het deze maand.**	He forgot this month.
Hij *ontdekte* **het te laat.**	He discovered it too late.
Sanne *geloofde* **het niet.**	Sanne didn't believe it.

The simple past tense for inseparable verbs follows the rules for regular and irregular verbs. The inseparable prefix has no influence on the formation of the past tense form.

The simple past of hebben **and** zijn

The singular form of the simple past for **hebben** is **had**, the plural form is **hadden**. The singular form for **zijn** is **was**, and the plural form is **waren**. Examples:

Erik *was* vandaag op zijn werk.	Erik was at work today.
Hij *had* een vervelende dag.	He had an annoying day.
Karin en Sanne *waren* in de stad.	Karin and Sanne were in town.
Zij *hadden* veel plezier.	They had a lot of fun.

The simple past forms of **hebben** and **zijn** are used much more frequently than the present perfect forms.

Some irregular forms

Some verbs don't follow either the rules for weak verbs or those for strong verbs or have other irregularities. Examples: **brengen** 'bring' ⇒ **bracht**, **denken** 'think' ⇒ **dacht**, **doen** 'do' ⇒ **deed**, **gaan** 'go' ⇒ **ging**, **kopen** 'buy' ⇒ **kocht**, **slaan** 'hit' ⇒ **sloeg**, **staan** 'stand' ⇒ **stond**, **weten** 'know' ⇒ **wist**, **zeggen** 'say' ⇒ **zei**, **zien** 'see' ⇒ **zag**, **zoeken** 'look for' ⇒ **zocht**. For more examples, check the Appendix in the back of this book.

The simple past of modal verbs

The simple past tense of sentences with modal verbs is formed by putting the modal verb into the simple past. Examples:

Sanne *wilde* een pot jam openen.
Sanne wanted to open a jar of jelly/jam.

Maar ze *kon* de deksel er niet af krijgen.
But she couldn't get the lid to come off.

Ze *moest* het even aan Erik vragen.
She had to ask Erik.

There is a singular and a plural form:

kunnen	*moeten*	*mogen*	*willen*	*zullen*
kon	**moest**	**mocht**	**wilde/wou**	**zou**
konden	**moesten**	**mochten**	**wilden/wouden**	**zouden**

Exercise 19.1

For each weak verb, decide whether the simple past form must end in
-de or **-te**.

1	werken 'work'	te	9	kloppen 'knock'	
2	studeren 'study'		10	lenen 'lend', 'borrow'	
3	bestellen 'order'		11	missen 'miss'	
4	drukken 'press', 'print'		12	openen 'open'	
5	gebeuren 'happen'		13	parkeren 'park'	
6	groeien 'grow'		14	roken 'smoke'	
7	hopen 'hope'		15	trouwen 'marry'	
8	huren 'rent'				

Exercise 19.2

In the text, underline all of the simple past tense forms and write down
their infinitive forms.

Situation: Erik reads the local paper. A robbery!

Inbraak (robbery) bij Juwelier Jansen. Gisteren is er bij Juwelier Jansen
op de Piet Heinstraat ingebroken. Volgens de politie brak de dief het
slot (lock) van de deur met een zwaar voorwerp (heavy object) en ging
vervolgens de winkel binnen zonder (without) het alarm te activeren. Hij
opende vier van de zes uitstalkasten (display cabinets) en stal voor
ongeveer 3 miljoen euro kostbare (valuable) juwelen. Een voorbijganger
(passer-by) zag de opengebroken deur en waarschuwde (warn) de politie.
Toen die arriveerde, was de dief al weg (gone). Waarom het alarm niet
functioneerde, is nog niet bekend (known). De juwelier beweerde (maintain) dat het alarm altijd goed werkte.
Verbs: _____

_____

_____

Exercise 19.3

Put the verbs into the simple past tense. (* = strong).

Situation: Erik's last vacation.

We (gaan*) _____ (1) met de auto naar Frankrijk. We (kamperen)
_____ (2) met twee tenten op vier verschillende campings. We

(eten*) _____ (3) elke dag verse croissants, heerlijk! We (zwemmen*) _____ (4) 's morgens in zee. We (wandelen) _____ (5) 's middags door de kleine dorpen. We (zitten*) _____ (6) vaak op een terrasje. We (praten) _____ (7) Frans met de buurman op de camping. Dat (zijn*) _____ (8) een arts uit Parijs. Hij (hebben*) _____ (9) drie kleine kinderen en een hond bij zich. Die hond (blaffen) _____ (10) je 's morgens uit je bed!

Exercise 19.4

Rewrite the sentences and put the modal verb in the simple past.

Situation: Erik thinks children are spoilt these days. Listen to how he was raised!

1 Wij hielpen altijd in het huishouden (moeten)

2 Wij speelden 's avonds nooit lang buiten (mogen)

3 Oma gaf ons maar heel weinig zakgeld (kunnen)

4 Opa hielp ons niet met ons huiswerk (willen)

5 Wij gingen nooit op vakantie (kunnen)

Exercise 19.5

Put the verbs between brackets in the simple past.

Situation: Looking at a new flat.

Gisteren (bekijken) _____ (1) ik een nieuwe woning. Het gebouw (liggen) _____ (2) in het centrum van de stad. De verhuurder (staan) _____ (3) al op mij te wachten bij de woning. Hij (laten) _____ (4) mij de woning van binnen zien. De woning (hebben) _____ (5) veel ruimte en licht. Ik (zien) _____ (6) ook een kelder onder het gebouw. De huur (zijn) _____ (7) zeshonderd euro per maand. Dat (vinden) _____ (8) ik wel een redelijke huurprijs. Maar je (mogen) _____ (9) in dat huis geen dieren hebben. Daarom (nemen) _____ (10) ik de woning niet.

Exercise 19.6

Put the underlined verbs into the simple past.

Situation: Sanne had a bad day.

Ik zit (1) in een café. Ik wacht (2) op Linda. Er komt (3) een man binnen. Hij gaat (4) bij mij aan het tafeltje zitten. Hij bestelt (5) bier. Hij steekt (6) een sigaret op. Ik zeg (7) iets tegen de ober. Je mag (8) daar namelijk niet roken. De ober vraagt (9) hem alstublieft buiten op het terras te roken. Die vent wordt (10) kwaad en gooit (11) zijn bier over mijn jurk. Gelukkig is (12) Linda er al. We rijden (13) meteen naar haar huis. Ze leent (14) me een jurk terwijl mijn jurk buiten in de wind hangt (15) te drogen. Wat een dag!

1 _____. 2 _____. 3 _____. 4 _____. 5 _____. 6 _____. 7 _____. 8 _____.
9 _____. 10 _____. 11 _____. 12 _____. 14 _____. 15 _____.

UNIT TWENTY
The imperative

Introduction

The imperative is the construction with which we give commands. While the form is easy to learn, the particles that accompany the imperative make it rather more complicated. Therefore, a special section of this unit is devoted to particles.

The forms

Singular, no subject	*Kom* **binnen.**	Come in.
	Neem **een koekje.**	Have a cookie.
Plural, no subject	*Komt* **binnen.**	Come in.
	Neemt **een koekje.**	Have a cookie.

The most common form of the imperative is simply the *stem* of the verb: **kom** 'come', **ga** 'go', **werk** 'work', **help** 'help', **denk na** 'think' (separable), **betaal** 'pay' (inseparable). This form can be used to address a single person or a group. When a group is addressed, sometimes a **-t** is added to the stem. But rather than using this old form, in the plural we prefer to add a subject. The verb conjugation follows the personal pronoun. Examples:

Singular, with subject	*Kom jij* **eens hier.**	Come here for a second.
	Neem jij **maar een koekje.**	Go ahead, have a cookie.
Plural, with subject	*Komen jullie* **eens binnen.**	Come in (all of you).
	Nemen jullie **maar een koekje.**	You all have a cookie.
Formal, with subject	*Komt u* **binnen.**	Come in (formal).
	Neemt u **toch een koekje.**	Please, have a cookie.

When the second person singular is added as a subject, it must be the emphasized form **jij**. The imperative form with the subject **u** can address more than one person.

Other forms

The *infinitive* of the verb, or an infinitive construction, is also used to give a command or prohibit something (examples 1–4 below). Lastly, the *past participle* or a participle construction may be used to give a command or advice, friendly or less friendly (examples 5–7).

1 **Niet *roken*!**	No smoking.
2 ***Doorhalen* wat niet van toepassing is.**	Cross out whatever doesn't apply.
3 **Niet *zeuren*, *dooreten*.**	Don't whine, keep eating.
4 ***Opschieten*!**	Hurry up!
5 **Nu *opgelet*, we gaan beginnen.**	Pay attention, we are starting.
6 ***Opgedonderd* jij!**	Get lost!
7 **Niet *getreurd*, we vinden wel een nieuwe.**	Don't cry, we'll find (you) a new one.

The imperative of the verb zijn

The imperative form of **zijn** is irregular, and it is conjugated as follows:

***Wees* voorzichtig, die camera is nieuw!**	Be careful, that camera is new.
***Weest* u maar niet bang.**	Please, don't be afraid.

Spelling

Verbs with stems ending in **-v-** or **-z-** end in **-f** and **-s** in the imperative: **geven – geef**, **lezen – lees**. In writing and in speech, verbs with stems ending in **-d** after a vowel often drop the **-d** in the imperative: **rijden – rij(d)**, **houden – hou(d)**.

The imperative modified by particles

The imperative can be modified by particles to make the command or suggestion sound friendlier, to express impatience, to express anger or irritation, or to express some form of resignation. Often the intonation used by the speaker indicates how a command is supposed to be understood. In the following overview, examples will be presented with the particles **eens**, **even**, **maar**, **toch**, **nou** and combinations of these.

eens, even, maar

The particle **eens** (often combined with **even**) gives the imperative a friendlier, milder tone. The particle **even** has a function very similar to **eens**. It makes the imperative friendlier, more casual, and it makes it sound as though it should take the listener no time or effort to carry out the command. The particle **maar** also makes the imperative much friendlier, and at the same time it gives it a tone of encouragement or permissiveness. It is often combined with **even**. Some examples:

Kom eens (even) hier.	Come here (for a minute), please.
Geef me even je pen.	Give me your pen for a minute.
Ga maar.	Okay, you can go.
Zet die koffers hier maar neer.	Just put those suitcases over here.

toch, nou

The particle **toch** can have different meanings. It can express friendly encouragement or impatience and irritation. Intonation plays an important role. The particle **nou** gives a command or request a definite flavor of impatience.

Kom toch binnen.	(friendly tone) Please come in.
Hou toch op. (unfriendly tone)	O, cut it out!
Wees toch een beetje voorzichtig!	Please do be a little careful!
Schiet nou op!	Hurry up, will you!

eens even, maar even, nou even, toch even

Often in the imperative we see a combination of different particles. The particles **eens**, **maar**, **nou** and **toch** are frequently combined with **even**, although it hardly changes the meaning. By itself, or in combination with others, the particle **even** makes the command sound less burdensome or time consuming. Examples:

Ga eens even opzij.	Please move out of the way for a minute.
Zet de tv eens even aan.	Please turn the TV on for me, will you?
Kom maar even mee.	Please follow me if you will.
Kleed u zich maar even uit.	Please go ahead and undress for a minute.
Help nou even.	Please help me (with impatience).
Eet nou even je bord leeg.	Finish your plate (with impatience).
Ga toch even mee.	Come along for a minute.
Help die man toch even.	Give that man a hand, please!

nou maar, nou toch

While **nou maar** makes the command sound friendlier or more permissive, **nou toch** expresses impatience and irritation. Examples:

Ga nou maar.	Please just go. (or: All right, you can go.)
Doe dat boek nou maar weg.	Please just put that book away.
Laat dat kind nou toch lekker spelen.	Oh, just let that child play if she wants to.
Hou nou toch eens op met zeuren.	Stop nagging around, please.

This is just a short impression of all the options one has with particles. Combinations of three or more are not out of the ordinary. Examples, translations as close as possible:

Ga *maar eens even* **kijken.**	Just go and take a quick look.
Ga *nou toch even* **kijken.**	You should go and take a quick look.
Ga *toch maar eens even* **kijken.**	You really should go and take a quick look.

Exercise 20.1

In the table, write the imperative form with no subject added to it. Follow the example. Remember that **-v-** and **-z-** turn into **-f** and **-s** at the end of a word.

geven	1 geef	vragen	5	pakken	9
doen	2	lezen	6	nemen	10
kijken	3	lopen	7	wachten	11
zeggen	4	zijn	8	schrijven	12

Exercise 20.2

Enter the correct verbs in the imperative.

Situation: Sanne gives Erik and the kids things to do around the house.
Verbs: **brengen, geven, zetten, halen, doen**.

1 Peter, _____ even alle handdoeken uit de badkamer.
2 _____ de vuile was maar in de wasmachine.
3 Erik, _____ de vuilniszak even voor me naar buiten.
4 Karin, _____ de planten maar even water.
5 Erik, _____ even een lekkere pot koffie.

Exercise 20.3

Enter the correct verbs in the imperative.

Situation: Reading a recipe for potato salad.

Verbs: **snijden** 'cut', **koken** 'boil', **schillen** 'peel', **mengen** 'mix', **zetten** 'put', 'place', **doen** 'do', 'put', **openen** 'open', **gieten** 'pour', **roeren** 'stir', **serveren** 'serve'.

1 _____ zes grote aardappels. 2 _____ de aardappels tot ze gaar maar nog stevig zijn. 3 _____ de aardappels in kleine stukjes. 4 _____ een blikje sperzieboontjes of doperwten. 5 _____ de boontjes of doperwten bij de aardappelstukjes. 6 _____ twee eetlepels mayonaise met wat olie en azijn, peper en dille. 7 _____ dit sausje over de salade. 8 _____ het sausje door het aardappelmengsel. 9 _____ de salade een uurtje in de koelkast. 10 _____ de salade met worst of gekookte eieren.

Exercise 20.4

Change the words between brackets into complete sentences in the imperative.

Situation: Sanne is ordering her family around while they are getting ready to leave for work and school.

1 Peter, (opschieten in de douche) _____
2 Karin, (het ontbijt klaarzetten) _____
3 Erik, (even de hond uitlaten) _____
4 Erik, (deze envelop even op de bus doen) _____
5 Peter, (je voetbalspullen meenemen) _____
6 Karin, (je lunch niet vergeten) _____
7 Erik, (deze jampot even openmaken) _____
8 Peter, (je mobiele telefoon uitdoen) _____
9 Karin, (me de boter even aangeven) _____
10 Peter en Karin, (om zes uur thuis zijn) _____

Exercise 20.5

Put the verbs into the imperative form. Sometimes it is formal.

Situation: After work, Erik and his friend Stefan are in a café. They talk about going to the movies tonight.

Ober:	(zeggen) _____ (1) u het maar.	
Erik:	(brengen) _____ (2) u mij een pilsje, alstublieft.	
Stefan:	(geven) _____ (3) u mij maar een jenever.	
	Hier Erik, (nemen) _____ (4) een sigaret van mij.	
Erik:	Nee dank je, (geven) _____ (5) mij maar een pepermuntje.	
Stefan:	(gaan) _____ (6) mee naar de film vanavond. Alhambra,	
	negen uur.	
	(vragen) _____ (7) even of Sanne ook mee wil.	
Erik:	Goed, maar (kopen) _____ (8) jij van te voren even de	
	kaartjes.	
Stefan:	Ja, maar (komen) _____ (9) niet te laat.	
Erik:	(zeuren) _____ (10) niet, ik kom nooit te laat.	

UNIT TWENTY-ONE
Reflexive verbs

Introduction

A reflexive verb is used to express an action that a person does to him- or herself. The *direct* object of a reflexive verb is the same person (or thing) as the subject, and the object pronoun is called a reflexive pronoun. Typical Dutch reflexive verbs are those that describe daily routines such as **zich wassen** 'to wash oneself', **zich scheren** 'to shave', **zich aankleden** 'to dress', and quite a few of them express a feeling or emotion or state of mind: **zich schamen** 'to be ashamed', **zich vervelen** 'to be bored', **zich ergeren** 'to be annoyed'. This chapter discusses 'true' reflexive verbs (they are always accompanied by a reflexive pronoun) and those that can also appear non-reflexive.

Conjugation of a reflexive verb

zich wassen to wash oneself

ik was *me*	myself	**wij/we wassen** *ons*	ourselves
jij/je wast *je*	yourself	**jullie wassen** *je*	yourselves
u wast *zich (u)*	yourself	**u wast** *zich (u)*	yourselves
hij, zij/ze, het wast *zich*	him/her/itself	**zij/ze wassen** *zich*	themselves

Note: The reflexive pronoun of the second person formal **u** can be either **zich** or **u**:

> **U moet zich haasten!** You have to hurry. Alternative: **U moet u haasten!**

The preferred form, however, is **zich**.

'True' reflexive verbs

A large number of reflexive verbs are a fixed combination of a verb and a reflexive pronoun. In Dutch they are called **noodzakelijk reflexief**, 'necessarily reflexive'.

Peter *schaamt zich* **voor zijn slechte cijfer.**
Peter is ashamed of his bad grade.

Annie *vergist zich* **in de datum.**
Annie is wrong about the date.

Karin *verslikt zich* **in haar snoepje.**
Karin nearly chokes on her candy.

Erik *haast zich* **naar de trein.**
Erik hurries to catch the train.

Die kinderen *gedragen zich* **slecht.**
Those children behave badly.

Bemoei je **met je eigen zaken!**
Mind your own business!

De student *bedronk zich* **op het feestje.**
The student got drunk at the party.

Erik haast zich naar de trein.

Some verbs can occur as 'true' reflexive verbs and as verbs without a reflexive pronoun. They are considered to be 'true' reflexive verbs when their meaning differs totally from the same verb without the reflexive pronoun. Note the difference between 1 and 2:

1 **Je moet** *je* **niet zo gek** *aanstellen.*   Don't make a fool of yourself.
2 **De chef** *stelt* **een nieuwe assistente**   The boss appoints a new
   aan.   assistant.

133

The verbs **zich aanstellen** and **aanstellen** are so different in meaning that the combination with the reflexive pronoun makes **zich aanstellen** a 'true' reflexive verb.

'Not necessarily reflexive' verbs

Many reflexive verbs are called **niet noodzakelijk**, 'not necessarily' reflexive verbs, because they can appear with or without a reflexive pronoun, and when the *direct* object is not a reflexive pronoun, the meaning of the verb is still related to the meaning of the same verb with the reflexive pronoun. Examples:

Ina wast *zich.*	Ina washes herself.
Ina wast *de baby.*	Ina washes the baby.
Erik scheert *zich* **met een apparaat.**	Erik shaves with an electric shaver.
De kapper scheert *zijn klant* **met het mes.**	The barber shaves his client with a razor.

Sometimes, the ending **-zelf** is added to a reflexive pronoun in combination with a 'not necessarily reflexive' verb, and only for the purpose of contrast. Examples:

Ina wast eerst *zichzelf* **en daarna de baby.**
Ina washes first herself and then the baby.

Hij bediende *zichzelf*, **niet zijn gasten.**
He served himself, not his guests.

For more examples on **zich** and **zelf**, check *Intermediate Dutch*. Many non-reflexive verbs are used with a reflexive pronoun in fixed expressions: **zich dood schrikken** 'be frightened to death', **zich slap lachen** 'laugh one's head off, **zich uit het naad werken** 'work extremely hard', **zich geen raad weten** 'not know what to do'.

The position of a reflexive pronoun in a sentence

In a coordinated sentence, the reflexive pronoun follows the conjugated verb (example 1). In a subordinated sentence, the reflexive pronoun follows the subject (example 2).

1 **Erik scheert *zich* elke dag.** Erik shaves every day.
2 **Geloof jij dat Erik *zich* elke dag** Do you believe Erik shaves every
  scheert? day?

Exercise 21.1

In these dialogues with 'true' reflexive verbs, enter the correct reflexive
pronoun.

    Erik: We moeten vandaag naar de tandarts, Sanne.
1 Sanne: Nee Erik, je vergist _____, we moeten donderdag pas.
    Erik: Wat heb je nu met je haar gedaan?!
2 Sanne: O, ik schaam _____ zo, ik heb het laten permanenten.
            Vreselijk, hè?
    Erik: Is het al tijd om naar de trein te gaan?
3 Sanne: Ja, het is al kwart voor acht, we moeten _____ haasten.
    Erik: Wat zijn dat vervelende kinderen!
4 Sanne: Kinderen kunnen _____ tegenwoordig niet gedragen.
    Erik: Hmm, lekker die vis!
5 Sanne: Pas op! Er kan een graatje ('bone') in zitten, verslik _____ niet.

Exercise 21.2

What is Erik doing in images 21.2 and 21.3? Write complete sentences.

1 _____   2 _____

Exercise 21.3

Complete the dialogues. Conjugate the verbs correctly, and enter the
reflexive pronouns.

1A: (zich voorstellen) Mag ik _____ even _____? Erik Beumer.
1B: Aangenaam. Kees Steenwijk.

2A: (zich amuseren) _____ u ____?

2B: O ja, het is een heel gezellig feest.

3A: Nog twee dagen werken en dan: vakantie!

3B: (zich verheugen) Ja, heerlijk, wij _____ zo op de zon en de zee!

4A: (zich vervelen) _____ jullie ____?

4B: Ja, het regent en we hebben binnen niks leuks te doen.

5A: Hoe gaat het met je vrouw?

5B: (zich voelen) Ze _____ niet zo lekker de laatste tijd.

6A: Goh, de benzine is al weer duurder geworden!

6B: (zich verbazen) _____ je _____ daarover? Alles wordt toch duurder!

7A: (zich herinneren) _____ jij _____ die keer dat Peter door het ijs gezakt is?

7B: O ja, vreselijk, wat was ik toen bang.

8A: Zeg, hoeveel salarisverhoging heb jij eigenlijk gekregen?

8B: (zich bemoeien) Ja zeg, _____ met je eigen zaken!

9A: Meneer Jansen, we hebben nu een vergadering.

9B: (zich vergissen) Nee, u _____, de vergadering is pas om drie uur.

10A: (zich scheren) _____ jij _____ nog met een mes?

10B: Nee, al lang niet meer. Ik heb een Philishave.

UNIT TWENTY-TWO
Infinitive constructions

Introduction

In Unit 2, five modal auxiliaries were introduced: **kunnen**, **moeten**, **mogen**, **willen**, **zullen**. This unit discusses two more groups of verbs with infinitives: those that have only an infinitive and those that have an infinitive combined with **te**.

laten

In its function of auxiliary, **laten** 'let' means 'having someone do something for you, rather than doing it yourself' (1), 'giving someone permission to do something' (2) or 'making a suggestion' (3). Examples:

1	**Sanne *laat* haar haar knippen.**	Sanne is having her hair cut.
2	**Peter *laat* Karin zijn computer gebruiken.**	Peter allows Karin to use his computer.
3	***Laten* we naar de bioscoop gaan.**	Let's go to the movies.

gaan, komen, blijven

The verb **gaan** expresses 'what someone plans to do, what is going to happen'(1–3). The verbs **komen** and **blijven** mean 'coming or staying to do something' (4, 5).

1	**Erik *gaat* even een brood kopen.**	Erik is going to buy a loaf of bread.
2	**Sanne, wat *ga* jij vanavond doen?**	Sanne, what are you going to do tonight?
3	**Ik blijf thuis, want het *gaat* regenen.**	I'm staying in, because it is going to rain.

4 **Cindy *komt* vanavond eten.**   Cindy is coming to dinner tonight.
5 **Peter *blijft* bij Johan slapen.**   Peter stays over at Johan's.

Note: The verb **gaan** in its function as an auxiliary is one of the most common forms of the future tense in Dutch.

horen, zien, voelen

As auxiliaries, these verbs mean that one can 'hear, see, or feel something happening'.

Erik *hoort* de buurman piano spelen.   Erik can hear the neighbor play the piano.
Peter *ziet* een kind de straat oversteken.   Peter watches a child cross the street.
Sanne *voelt* een storm aankomen.   Sanne can feel a storm approaching.

Present Perfect

In the present perfect, all these verbs move to the end of the sentence as infinitives, and either **hebben** or **zijn** is used as the auxiliary verb. Examples:

Sanne <u>heeft</u> haar haar *laten knippen*.   Sanne had her hair cut.
Peter <u>is</u> *gaan voetballen*.   Peter went to play soccer.
<u>Heb</u> je Nureyev wel eens *zien dansen*?   Did you ever see Nureyev dance?
Wanneer <u>ben</u> je hier *komen wonen*?   When did you move here?
Katja <u>is</u> gisteren *blijven eten*.   Katja stayed for dinner yesterday.

zijn

Common only in situations where someone has to actually leave the house to go to do something in a different location, **zijn** can be used as an auxiliary verb with an infinitive (1). It is similar to the English '-ing' form. The present perfect of such constructions (2) is not with the past participle **geweest**, but with **wezen**. Examples:

1 **Waar is Erik? Die *is* vissen.**   Where is Erik? He's fishing.
2 **Erik *is* gisteren *wezen* vissen.**   Erik went fishing yesterday.

Verbs with an infinitive and te

A substantial group of verbs is combined with an infinitive and **te**, similar to English 'I try *to study*' (**Ik probeer te studeren**) or 'I forgot *to* bring my umbrella' (**Ik vergat mijn paraplu mee te brengen**). Note that in *separable verbs*, **te** separates the prefix from the main verb (**uit *te* laten**). Some examples:

beginnen te	'begin'/'start to'	**beloven te**	'promise to'
durven te	'dare to'	**hopen te**	'hope to'
verbieden te	'prohibit'	**vergeten te**	'forget to'
besluiten te	'decide to'	**weigeren te**	'refuse to'
proberen te	'try to'		

Erik begint *te werken*.	Erik starts to work.
Karin durft geen haring *te eten*.	Karin doesn't dare to eat herring.
Erik probeert de auto *te repareren*.	Erik tries to repair the car.
Peter vergeet de hond *uit te laten*.	Peter forgets to walk the dog.

zitten, staan, liggen, lopen, hangen

These verbs are used to form 'durative constructions', meaning that someone is, for example, actually sitting or standing while doing something. Examples:

Sanne *zit* op de bank een boek *te lezen*.	Sanne is reading a book on the sofa.
Erik *staat* op de markt een haring *te eten*.	Erik is eating a herring at the market.

The present perfect of these durative constructions is formed with the auxiliary verb **hebben** and two infinitives, the infinitive of the main or independent verb last. The two infinitives may or may not be separated by **te**.

Karin *heeft* haar telefoon *lopen (te) zoeken*.	Karin was looking for her phone.
Peter *heeft* naar de tv *liggen (te) kijken*.	Peter was watching TV.

schijnen, blijken

The verb **schijnen** is used when the speaker has some information but isn't sure whether that information is correct. In this modality, the verb

lijken is also used. If the speaker is certain, the verb **blijken** is preferred. Examples:

1 **De leraar** *schijnt/lijkt* **ziek te zijn.**   The teacher appears (seems) to be ill.
2 **De leraar** *blijkt* **ziek te zijn.**   The teacher is evidently ill.

In sentence 1, we assume the teacher is ill because he hasn't come to work and we think he might be ill. In sentence 2, the teacher has called in sick and we know for sure. The verbs **schijnen**, **lijken** and **blijken** also often appear with a subordinated sentence with **dat** or **alsof**. Examples:

Het lijkt *alsof* **de leraar ziek is.**   It looks like the teacher is ill.
Het schijnt *dat* **de leraar ziek is.**   It seems that the teacher is ill.
Het is gebleken *dat* **de leraar ziek is.**   It is obvious that the teacher is ill.

Verbs with or without te: helpen, leren

Some infinitive constructions can appear with or without **te**. There is a preference for **te** when the sentence is longer because of a direct object or other sentence elements. Examples:

Karin *helpt* **Sanne koken.**	Karin is helping Sanne with the cooking.
Karin *helpt* **Sanne het eten** *te* **koken.**	Karin is helping Sanne to cook dinner.
Hij *leert* **mij dansen.**	He teaches me to dance.
Hij *leert* **mij de tango** *te* **dansen.**	He teaches me to dance the tango.

In the present perfect, the verbs **helpen** and **leren** can use a past participle (1) or a double infinitive (2) and keep or drop **te** (3).

1 **Karin heeft Sanne geholpen het eten te koken.**
2 **Karin heeft Sanne helpen koken.**
3 **Karin heeft Sanne het eten helpen (te) koken.**

A special case: hoeven (niet hoeven te)

The verb **hoeven** almost always appears with the negation adverb **niet**, and its function is to give a negative answer to a question with **moeten**. Note again that **te** separates the prefix from the stem of a separable verb. Examples:

Moet ik dat doen? Nee, dat <u>hoef</u> je *niet* <u>te</u> doen.
Do I have to do that? No, you don't have to do that.

Moeten we onze atlassen meebrengen? Nee, jullie hoeven je atlassen *niet* <u>mee te brengen</u>.
Do we have to bring our atlasses? No, you don't have to bring your atlasses.

The present perfect of verbs with te + infinitive

Most of the infinitives with **te** form their present perfect with the past participle of the verb and the infinitive construction at the end of the sentence (1 and 2). Some verbs, on the other hand, form the present perfect with an auxiliary and two infinitives. Sometimes, **te** is optional (3 and 4). Some verbs form the present perfect both ways (5 and 6).

1	**beginnen:**	**Erik *is begonnen* te werken.**	Erik has started to work.
2	**verbieden:**	**Ik *heb* je *verboden* hier te roken.**	I forbade you to smoke here.
3	**durven:**	**Ik heb het niet *durven (te) doen.***	I didn't dare to do it.
4	**hoeven:**	**Ik heb het niet *hoeven (te) doen.***	I didn't have to do it.
5	**proberen:**	**Ik heb *geprobeerd* hem te helpen.**	I tried to help him.
6	**proberen:**	**Ik heb hem *proberen* te helpen.**	I tried to help him.

Infinitive constructions with om . . . te . . .

Infinitive constructions with **om . . . te . . .** are used in the following situations: 1 when there is a clear sense of purpose, a goal, a reason why something happens or why someone does something; 2 to express the function of an object, the reason why it is used, and 3 after an adjective with **te**, for example **te groot** 'too big'.

1 **Ik ga naar de bakker *om* brood *te* kopen.**
   I go to the bakery to buy bread.

2 **Dit glas is *om* witte wijn uit *te* drinken.**
   This glass is for drinking white wine.

3 **Die tas is *te zwaar om te* dragen.**
   That bag is too heavy to carry.

Infinitive constructions after a predicate adjective

An infinitive with **te** also follows a predicate adjective used in sentences such as **het is leuk . . .**, **het is moeilijk . . .**, **ik vind het vervelend . . .**, and the like. Examples:

Het is *leuk* **een film** *te zien.*	It is fun to watch a movie.
Nederlands is *moeilijk te leren.*	Dutch is hard to learn.

In speech, **om** is often added to these infinitive constructions. Some of the verbs with an infinitive + **te** as discussed above are used with **om** in spoken (not in written) Dutch.

Ik vind het leuk (om) naar de film te gaan.
I like going to the movies.

Peter heeft geprobeerd (om) Johan op te bellen.
Peter tried to phone Johan.

Sanne heeft besloten (om) een nieuwe tv te kopen.
Sanne has decided to buy a new TV.

The expression zin om . . . te . . .

When the Dutch want to say 'I would like to do this or that', they use the expression **zin om . . . te . . .** 'the desire to . . .' with an infinitive. The expression is negated with **geen**.

Ik heb *zin om* **naar de film** *te* **gaan.**	I would like to go to the movies.
Sanne heeft *geen zin om te* **koken.**	Sanne doesn't feel like cooking.

Exercise 22.1

Give a negative answer to each question using **Nee, je hoeft . . . niet/geen . . . te . . . .**

Situation: Erik is with his family doctor. It's not a very stressful visit.

	Erik:	Moet ik m'n kleren uittrekken?
1	Dokter:	Nee, je _____
	Erik:	Moet ik een bloedtest doen?
2	Dokter:	_____
	Erik:	Moet ik medicijnen nemen?

3 Dokter: _____
  Erik: Moet ik weer terugkomen?
4 Dokter: _____
  Erik: Moet ik meteen voor dit consult betalen?
5 Dokter: _____
  Erik: Dank u wel. Dag, dokter.

Exercise 22.2

Complete the sentences with an infinitive construction with **om ... te ...**
using the underlined words.

Situation: Erik is in a bad mood. He complains about everything.

  Sanne: Wil je <u>in de tuin werken</u>?
1 Erik: Ah, ik ben te moe _____.
  Sanne: Zullen we even koffie <u>drinken</u>?
2 Erik: Bah, deze koffie is te slap _____.
  Sanne: Ga je vanmiddag <u>tennis spelen</u>?
3 Erik: Het is te warm _____.
  Sanne: Laten we even <u>naar het nieuws kijken</u>.
4 Erik: Ik vind het zo vervelend _____.
  Sanne: <u>Lees</u> dan het nieuwe boek van Mulisch.
5 Erik: Ach, dat boek is veel te dik _____.

Exercise 22.3

What are they doing and why? Finish the sentence with an infinitive construction with **om ... te ....**.

Situation: What is the family doing this weekend?

1 Erik gaat naar de autowasstraat (de auto laten wassen) _____
  _____

2 Sanne schrijft een email (haar vriendin voor het eten uitnodigen) ____
  _____

3 Peter gaat naar de sportwinkel (naar nieuwe voetbalschoenen kijken)
  _____

4 Karin zoekt haar mobiele telefoon (haar vriendin Katja opbellen) ____
  _____

5 Erik en Sanne gaan naar een concert (Placido Domingo horen zingen)
  _____

6 Karin gaat naar Katja (samen huiswerk maken) _____
  _____

Exercise 22.4

An exercise with modal auxiliaries. Change the sentences for Peter's answers using the modal verbs and adverbs given between the brackets.

Sanne: Heb je je huiswerk al gemaakt?
1 Peter: (nog moeten) Nee, ik _____
Erik: Kijk je vanavond naar de voetbalwedstrijd?
2 Peter: (niet willen) Nee, ik _____
Karin: Help je me even met wiskunde?
3 Peter: (niet kunnen) Nee, ik _____
Sanne: Eet je vanavond thuis?
4 Peter: (blijven) Ja, ik _____
Erik: Wil je je koffie boven drinken?
5 Peter: (beneden komen) Nee, ik _____

Exercise 22.5

Put the sentences into the present perfect.

Situation: Last night at the Beumers.

1 Karin probeert een vriendin te bellen.

_____

2 Johan komt Peter met zijn wiskunde helpen.

_____

3 Johan blijft bij de Beumers eten.

_____

4 Erik zit de krant te lezen.

_____

5 Sanne laat Erik de aardappels schillen.

_____

Exercise 22.6

Put the words in the correct order, beginning with proper names: first the modal auxiliary, then the verb that can be used as such (with or without **te**), and then the main verb.

1 horen – de buurman – Sanne – zingen – kunnen

_____

2 de accu van de auto – laten – Erik – moeten – opladen

_____

3 Karin – eten – bij een vriendin – vanavond – blijven – willen

_____

4 komen – over een probleem – mogen – bij de rector – Peter – praten

_____

5 met een vriend – vissen – gaan – Erik – morgenochtend – willen

_____

UNIT TWENTY-THREE
Word order

Introduction

This unit offers an overview of basic Dutch word order in three sections. Section 1 discusses word order in basic, coordinated sentences. Section 2 continues with word order in subordinated clauses. The unit ends with Section 3, word order in indirect speech. Each section has examples of conjunctions, the words that link clauses together.

Section 1: word order in main clauses

To form a complete grammatical sentence, one needs two elements: a verb and a subject:

> **Erik** *werkt.*   Erik works (is working).

Other elements can be added: adverbs of time, a place, objects, prepositional phrases. Note the stability of the subject–verb position in the examples:

Erik *werkt* **hard.**	Erik works hard.
Erik *werkt* **op zaterdag hard.**	Erik works hard on Saturday.
Erik *werkt* **op zaterdag in de tuin.**	Erik works in the garden on Saturday.
Erik *werkt* **op zaterdag met Sanne in de tuin.**	Erik works in the garden with Sanne on Saturday.

In a main clause (Dutch: **hoofdzin**), the conjugated verb takes the second position. All other sentence parts follow the subject verb group. Within the other sentence parts, the word order is not arbitrary, but follows the model *time, manner, place.* See how the sentence **Erik gaat**

vandaag met de auto naar z'n werk 'Erik is going to work by car today' is organized in the following sentence parts:

Subject	Verb	Time	Manner	Place
Erik	**gaat**	**vandaag**	**met de auto**	**naar z'n werk.**

This basic word order changes in the following situations:

a When the subject is not the first part of the sentence, the verb stays in second position, and the subject moves to the third. This is called *inversion* of subject and verb. Example:

   Vandaag *gaat* Erik met de auto naar z'n werk.

b When the sentence is a yes/no question, the verb moves to the first position:

   ***Gaat* Erik vandaag met de auto naar z'n werk?**

c When the sentence is in the command form, it begins with the verb:

   ***Kom* vanavond naar ons feestje!**   Come to our party tonight!

In main sentences with transitive verbs (verbs that can have a direct object), the indirect object is placed before the direct object. Example:

Erik geeft Sanne een bos bloemen.   Erik gives Sanne a bunch of flowers.
Peter vertelt Johan een mop.   Peter tells Johan a joke.

Sanne is the *indirect object* (the one to whom something happens), and **een bos bloemen** is the *direct object*. The word order stays the same, when **Sanne** is a pronoun:

Erik geeft *haar* een bos bloemen.   Erik gives *her* a bunch of flowers.

If the direct object is reduced to the personal pronoun **het**, the direct object precedes the indirect object. Examples:

Peter geeft haar het boek.   ⇒   **Peter geeft *het* haar.**
Peter gives it to her.

Ik vertel jou het verhaal niet!   ⇒   **Ik vertel *het* jou niet!**
I won't tell it to you.

Note: When the indirect object is preceded by a preposition, it can follow the direct object. Indeed, in speech we prefer this version:

Section 1: word order in main clauses

147

Peter geeft een boek *aan* Karin.
Ik ga even een glas wijn *voor* u
inschenken.

Peter gives Karin a book.
I'm going to pour you a glass of
wine.

In main sentences with auxiliary verbs, the auxiliary is the conjugated verb
in the second place, while the infinitive group or past participle moves to
the end of the sentence.

Erik *kan* met de trein naar z'n werk <u>gaan</u>.
Erik *is* vandaag met de auto naar z'n
werk <u>gegaan</u>.
Sanne *wil* vandaag haar haar <u>laten</u>
<u>knippen</u>.

Erik can go to work by train.
Erik went to work by car
today.
Sanne wants to have a hair cut
today.

Conjunctions link clauses together. Conjunctions linking a main clause
with another main clause are **en** 'and', **maar** 'but', **want** 'because', **of** 'or'.
Examples:

Erik werkt vandaag in de tuin *en* hij gaat naar de markt.
Erik is working in the garden today, and he is going to the market.

Sanne wil naar de kapper, *maar* de kapper is vandaag gesloten.
Sanne wants to go to the hairdresser, but the hairdresser is closed today.

Peter belt Johan op, *want* hij wil met hem huiswerk maken.
Peter calls Johan, because he wants to do homework with him.

Gaan we dit jaar naar Engeland op vakantie, *of* gaan we naar
Frankrijk?
Are we going to England on vacation this year or are we going to France?

Section 2: word order in subordinated clauses

In a subordinated clause (Dutch: **bijzin**), the conjugated verb moves to
the end of the clause. Many conjunctions can begin a subordinated clause.
In the following examples, the underlined clauses are subordinated:

Karin blijft thuis *<u>omdat</u> ze ziek is.
Karin stays home because she is sick.

Peter had een hondje *<u>toen</u> hij jong was*.
Peter had a little dog when he was young.

Sanne telefoneert met haar vriendin *<u>terwijl</u> ze koffie zet*.
Sanne is on the phone to her friend while she is making coffee.

Erik voelt zich veel fitter _sinds hij niet meer rookt_.
Erik feels much fitter since he stopped smoking.

Section 2:
word
order in
sub-
ordinated
clauses

When the order of the main and the subordinated clause is reversed, the main clause (*now beginning with the verb*) is separated from the subordinated clause by a comma:

Omdat ze ziek _is, blijft_ Karin thuis.
Toen hij jong _was, had_ Peter een klein hondje.
Terwijl ze koffie _zet, telefoneert_ Sanne met haar vriendin.
Sinds hij niet meer _rookt, voelt_ Erik zich veel fitter.

Note that when the sentence begins with a subordinated clause, the verb of the main clause follows the subordinated clause directly (i.e. an entire clause can take the first position in the sentence). The verbs of the two clauses are on each side of the comma.

In subordinated sentences in the *present perfect* tense, the auxiliary verb **hebben** or **zijn** can be on either side of the past participle. It is more common, however, to put the conjugated auxiliary verb before the past participle. Examples:

Peter is moe omdat hij hard *heeft* getraind.
Peter is tired because he trained hard.

Sanne ziet er mooi uit omdat ze naar de kapper *is* geweest.
Sanne looks beautiful because she was at the hairdresser's.

In subordinated sentences with **modal auxiliary verbs**, we prefer to put the conjugated modal verb before the infinitive at the end of the sentence. Examples:

Karin eet graag nootjes als ze *moet* studeren, omdat ze dan beter *kan* denken.
Karin likes to eat nuts when she has to study, because she can think better that way.

If the subordinated sentence with a modal verb contains a separable verb, the modal verb can be placed before the infinitive of the separable verb, or it can split it. Examples:

Karin pakt haar telefoon, omdat ze Sonja *wil* opbellen.
Karin takes her cell phone, because she wants to call Sonja.
Alternative: **Karin pakt haar telefoon, omdat ze Sonja op *wil* bellen.**

Section 3: word order in indirect speech

In indirect speech, a statement or question is repeated by someone other than the speaker who initiated the statement or question. Typically, an indirect statement begins with the conjunction **dat**, and indirect questions can begin with a question word, or, if the question was a yes–no–question, with **of**. Indirect statements are often introduced with verbs such as **zeggen** 'say', **menen** 'think', **denken** 'think', **beweren** 'maintain', and indirect questions might be introduced with words such as **hij/zij vraagt** 'he/she asks', **ik wil weten...** 'I want to know...' or **kun je me vertellen ...** 'can you tell me...'. Sentences in indirect speech are subordinated sentences; the conjugated verb moves to the end. Examples:

Erik:	Het wordt vandaag een mooie dag.
	It's going to be a beautiful day.
Sanne:	Erik zegt _dat_ het vandaag een mooie dag wordt.
Karin:	Ik heb zin in een hamburger.
	I would like to eat a hamburger.
Peter:	Karin zegt _dat ze zin in een hamburger heeft_.
Mvr. A:	Is dit de bus naar Workum?
	Is this bus going to Workum?
Mnr. B:	Mevrouw vraagt _of_ dit de bus naar Workum is.
Erik:	Waar liggen m'n sigaretten?
	Where are my cigarettes?
Sanne:	Erik wil weten _waar_ z'n sigaretten liggen.

Check also _Intermediate Dutch_ for indirect speech in more complicated sentence structures.

Exercise 23.1

Put the words in the correct order. Every sentence begins with the subject.

1 met Sanne/Erik/naar de markt/vandaag/gaat

_____

2 een haring/elke zaterdag/Erik/bij visboer Stegeman/eet

_____

3 vraagt/de aardbeien/Sanne/de groenteman/kosten/wat

_____

4 zin/een kop koffie/heeft/om/Sanne/te drinken

_____

5 om twaalf uur/zijn/bij de kapper/Erik/moet

_____

Exercise 23.2

Change the word order of each sentence by beginning with a different sentence part.

1 Peter speelt op zaterdag altijd voetbal.
  Op zaterdag _____
2 Hij fietst om negen uur met Johan naar de voetbalclub.
  Om negen uur _____
3 De jongens doen eerst met de trainer een lange warm-up.
  Met de trainer _____
4 Ze spelen na de warm-up in twee teams een oefenwedstrijdje.
  Na de warm-up _____
5 Johan en Peter fietsen meestal rond twaalf uur weer naar huis.
  Meestal _____

Exercise 23.3

Connect the two sentences using the conjunction provided.

Situation: Erik and Sanne in Paris.

1 Erik en Sanne waren in Parijs. Ze gingen naar het Louvre (toen).
  _____
2 Ze aten veel croissants. Ze dronken de beste café au lait (en).
  _____
3 Ze gingen naar Montmartre. Het weer was slecht op die dag (maar).
  _____
4 Sanne wilde naar de Eiffeltoren. Ze wilde panoramafoto's maken
  (omdat).
  _____
5 Sanne maakte foto's. Erik praatte met een andere Nederlandse toerist
  (terwijl).
  _____

Exercise 23.4

Put the sentences into indirect speech.

Situation: Erik phones from Paris. Peter tells Karin what Erik says.

Erik: "Het weer is bijna altijd goed."
1 Peter: Hij zegt _____
Erik: "Het was heel druk in het Louvre."
2 Peter: Hij zegt _____
Erik: "Mama maakt fantastische foto's."
3 Peter: Hij zegt _____
Erik: "Hoe gaat het thuis?"
4 Peter: Hij vraagt _____
Erik: "Lopen jullie twee keer per dag met de hond?"
5 Peter: Hij vraagt _____

UNIT TWENTY-FOUR
Relative clauses

Introduction

A relative clause begins with a relative pronoun and ends with a verb (it is a subordinated clause). The relative pronoun refers to a noun or other word earlier in the sentence (the antecedent). The relative clause gives information about the antecedent.

Examples

De man *die* daar zit, heet Erik. De vrouw *die* naast hem zit, heet Sanne. Erik leest een boek *dat* heel spannend is. Sanne bekijkt foto's *die* ze in Parijs gemaakt heeft. De foto *waarnaar* ze nu kijkt, is van de Eiffeltoren. De telefoon gaat. De persoon met *wie* Sanne nu praat, is haar vriendin Netty. Netty komt even koffiedrinken, *wat* Sanne heel leuk vindt.

The man who is sitting over there is Erik. The woman sitting next to him is Sanne. The book that Erik is reading is very thrilling. Sanne is looking at photos that she took in Paris. The photo she is looking at right now is of the Eiffel Tower. The phone rings. The person to whom Sanne is talking now is her friend Netty. Netty is coming over for coffee, something which Sanne really likes.

Relative pronouns

die	refers to de-words in the singular
dat	refers to het-words in the singular
die	refers to all nouns in the plural
waar + preposition	refers to objects preceded by a preposition[1]
wie	refers to persons preceded by a preposition[2]
wat	refers to a complete sentence; after indefinite pronouns[3]

1 The relative pronouns **die** and **dat** cannot refer to a word that is preceded by a preposition. This happens often in a sentence with a fixed
combination of verb and preposition such as **praten over** 'talk about',
denken aan 'think about', **kijken naar** 'look at', and with coincidental
combinations of verb and preposition. Examples:

Het land *waaraan* **ik denk, is mooi.**
The country I am thinking about is beautiful.

Het huis *waarin* **ik woon, is oud.**
The house in which I live is old.

The prepositions **met** and **tot** change into **mee** and **toe** when used in
combination with **waar-** to form a relative pronoun:

De pen *waarmee* **ik schrijf, is zwart.**
The pen with which I am writing is black.

Wat is het doel *waartoe* **dit object dient?**
What is the purpose of this object?

Lastly, the combination **waar** + preposition is often separated, and the
preposition is placed directly before the verb. Compare the following
pairs of sentences:

Het land *waaraan* **ik denk, is mooi. Het land** *waar* **ik** *aan* **denk, is mooi.**
Het huis *waarin* **ik woon, is oud. Het huis** *waar* **ik** *in* **woon, is oud.**
De pen *waarmee* **ik schrijf, is zwart. De pen** *waar* **ik** *mee* **schrijf, is
zwart.**

2 When the relative pronoun refers to a person preceded by a preposition, it must be **wie** rather than **die**. Examples:

De man met *wie* **Erik praat, heet Oscar.**
The man to whom Erik is talking is Oscar.

Dat is mijn wiskundeleraar, van *wie* **ik altijd slechte cijfers krijg.**
That is my math teacher, who always gives me bad grades.

3 The relative pronoun **wat** refers to a complete sentence, a fact that was
stated earlier. It also follows indefinite pronouns such as **iets**, **niets**, **alles**,
veel, **weinig**.

De winkel was al gesloten, <u>wat</u> **ik heel vervelend vond.**
The store was already closed, something I found very annoying.

Alles <u>wat</u> **je hier ziet, komt uit het huis van mijn grootouders.**
Everything you see here comes from my grandparents' home.

Er is *niets* <u>wat</u> **Erik niet lekker vindt.**
There is nothing that Erik doesn't like to eat.

Exercise 24.1

Underline the <u>relative pronoun</u> in the sentence.

1 Erik praat met z'n vriend Oscar, die in Engeland woont.
2 De vriend vertelt over het huis dat hij vorig jaar gekocht heeft.
3 Hij vertelt ook over de vrouw met wie hij nu getrouwd is.
4 Erik vertelt over het bedrijf waarvoor hij nu werkt.
5 Hij vertelt ook over zijn kinderen, die al naar de middelbare school gaan.

Exercise 24.2

Is the sentence correct or wrong, **goed** or **fout**?

1 Sanne zoekt vruchten dat ze wil kopen.	goed – fout
2 Ze ziet aardbeien die niet zo duur zijn.	goed – fout
3 De groenteman die ze fruit bij koopt, heeft het beste fruit.	goed – fout
4 De appels waarvan Sanne twee kilo koopt, zijn rood en zoet.	goed – fout
5 Sanne zet de aardbeien, die vanavond in de yoghurt gaan, in de koelkast.	goed – fout

Exercise 24.3

Fill in the correct relative pronoun. Select from: **die**, **dat**, **wie**, **wat**.

Situation: Sanne and Lydia gossip about a friend's neighbors.

1 Sanne: Ken jij die vrouw _____ nu naast Myriam woont?
2 Lydia: O ja, in het huis _____ voor vier ton verkocht is.
3 Sanne: Ze hebben twee auto's, _____ ik belachelijk vind.
4 Lydia: Ja, en een hond _____ elke week naar de hondenkapper moet!
5 Sanne: Nee! Wat doet die man met _____ ze getrouwd is?
6 Lydia: Hij werkt voor een firma _____ microchips maakt, geloof ik.
7 Sanne: Ze hebben een zoon _____ bij Peter in de klas zit.
8 Lydia: Nou, dan is er veel _____ hij je kan vertellen!
9 Sanne: Zeg, hoe vind je de koekjes _____ ik gisteren gebakken heb?
10 Lydia: Heerlijk. Mag ik het recept _____ je hebt gebruikt?
   Sanne: Dat heb ik van het internet.

Exercise 24.4

Turn the information between brackets into relative sentences.

Situation: Karin is in love with a boy from a different class and her friend Petra is trying to find out who it is.

1 Petra: Is het die jongen (hij zit naast Marco)?
_____ Karin: Nee!
2 Petra: Of is het die jongen (Kees speelt altijd tennis met hem)?
_____ Karin: Hoe kom je erbij?
3 Petra: O, dan is het die jongen met dat haar (het is totaal slecht geblondeerd)?
_____ Karin: Ook niet!
4 Petra: Ik weet het! Het is die vent (hij zit altijd met Elly te flirten).
_____ Karin: Nee, die is zo stom.
5 Petra: Aaah, jij bent verliefd op Simon (ik snap dat echt niet).
_____ Karin: O nee? Ik vind hem leuk.

Exercise 24.5

Turn the information between brackets into a relative clause. Note the prepositions.

Situation: Karin is selecting pictures for a class presentation about Anne Frank.

1 Dit is het boekje (ze schreef er haar notities in) _____

2 Hier zie je de boekenkast (er zat een trap achter) _____

3 Dit waren plaatjes en foto's (Anne maakte er haar kamer gezellig mee)

4 Dit was Fritz Pfeffer, een huisgenoot (Anne had een grote hekel aan hem) _____

5 Dit is Otto Frank, haar vader (Anne leerde heel veel van hem) _____

UNIT TWENTY-FIVE
Prepositions

Introduction

The function of prepositions is to create a relationship between sentence elements. They usually appear before a noun or a pronoun or another sentence part, and often they are part of a fixed expression, as when a verb or an adverb takes a certain preposition (**denken** *aan* 'think about', **bang** *voor* 'afraid of'). This unit discusses the most common types of relationships between prepositions and other sentence elements: time, manner or means, place or direction, cause or reason, and possession.

Examples in context

Erik gaat *om* acht uur *naar* zijn werk. Hij gaat meestal *met* de auto. Zijn bureau is *in* de stad. Hij werkt *bij* een grote firma. *Vanwege* het slechte weer neemt hij vandaag de trein. Erik ergert zich *aan* de drukte.
Erik goes *to* work *at* eight o'clock (time, direction). Usually he goes *by* car (manner, means). His office is *in* the city (place). He works *at* a large firm (place). *Because of* the bad weather he is taking the train today (reason, cause). Erik is annoyed *by* the crowd (verb with preposition).

Prepositions expressing time

na	after	**om**	at	**onder**	during	**over**	in
rond	around	**sinds**	since	**tegen**	just before	**tijdens**	during
tot	until	**tussen**	between	**van(af)**	from	**voor**	before

Sinds **een jaar zit Peter op de middelbare school. Hij moet 's morgens** *om* **half acht de deur uit, want hij fietst naar school.** *Na* **school fietst hij meestal meteen naar huis, want hij maakt zijn huiswerk** *voor* **het** eten. De Beumers eten meestal *rond* half zeven. *Onder* het eten praten ze over school en werk. *Tegen* acht uur zet Erik de televisie aan, omdat het journaal *over* een paar minuten begint. *Tijdens* het journaal drinken ze koffie. *Van* half negen *tot* half tien maakt Peter de rest van z'n huiswerk. Hij gaat meestal *tussen* half tien en tien uur naar bed.

Peter has been going to high school *for* a year. He has to leave the house *at* 7.30 in the morning, because he bikes to school. *After* school he usually bikes home right away, because he does his homework *before* dinner. The Beumer family usually eat dinner *around* 6.30 pm. *At* dinner, they talk about school and work. *Just before* eight, Erik turns on the television, because the news will begin *in* a few minutes. *During* the news, they drink coffee. *From* 8.30 *until* 9.30, Peter does the rest of his homework. He usually goes to bed *between* 9.30 and 10.00 pm.

dag, week, maand, jaar

in in   **op** on   **over** in   **per** per

In 1998 is Peter met voetbal begonnen. Hij traint twee keer *per* week, *op* maandag en donderdag. Hij heeft *op* 6 april een belangrijke wedstrijd. En dan is er een toernooi in mei. *In* die week heeft Peter weinig tijd voor school. *Over* een paar jaar gaat Peter naar de B-junioren.

In 1998, Peter started with soccer. He trains twice a week, *on* Mondays and Thursdays. *On* April 6, he has an important match. And then there is a tournament *in* May. *In* that week, Peter won't have much time for school. *In* a few years, Peter will move up to the B-juniors.

Note: English-speaking students of Dutch often mix up the **op** and **om** in time expressions. The preposition **om** is for clock time (**om vier uur, om half twee**), and the preposition **op** is for days of the week and dates (**op maandag, op 1 juli**). For more information, see Unit 5, Telling the time.

Prepositions expressing place

This is probably the largest group of prepositions. In this unit, they are divided into two categories: prepositions expressing motion in a certain direction, and those that just say something about the location of things or people. The section ends with a few notes on double prepositions.

Motion and direction

bij	at, near	**door**	through
over	over, across	**tot**	until, to
langs	along	**naar**	to
uit/van	out of, from	**voorbij**	past

Read the dialogue:

**Mevrouw A: Pardon meneer, ik kom net *uit* het museum en nu wil ik
naar het Centraal Station. Hoe kom ik daar?**
**Meneer B: U wilt *naar* het station? Dan moet u hier rechtdoor lopen
tot de hoek van deze straat. Daar gaat u rechtsaf. U loopt *langs* de gracht.
Bij de Rembrandtstraat moet u *naar* links. U loopt *over* de brug, dan
door het park en *voorbij* het monument. Dan steeds maar rechtdoor
en u komt vanzelf *bij* het station.**
Ms A: Excuse me, sir, I just came *from* the museum and now I want
to go *to* the Central Station. How do I get there?
Mr B: You want to go *to* the station? Then from here you must go straight
to the corner of the street. There you turn right. You walk *along* the
canal. At Rembrandtstraat, you go *to* the left. You walk *over* the
bridge, *through* the park and *past* the monument. Then keep going straight
and you'll automatically get *to* the station.

The most commonly used preposition to express motion to a place is **naar**,
mostly with the verb **gaan**. People go **naar het buro** 'to the office', **naar
de film** 'to the movies', **naar Amsterdam** 'to Amsterdam', **naar school** 'to
school', **naar bed** 'to bed', etc.

The preposition **uit** in motion is commonly used when you are saying
what country or city you are from (**Ik kom uit Groningen, uit Nederland**
'I'm from Groningen, from the Netherlands') or when you are coming out
of a building (**uit het museum**) or when something is taken out of a con-
tainer of some sort (**ik drink uit een glas** 'I drink from a glass', **ik pak een
koekje uit de trommel** 'I take a cookie from the tin'). The preposition **van**
is also used to refer to a place: **Ik kom net van school** 'I just came from
school'.

The preposition **bij** in motion is only used with the verb **komen**, referring
to people as well as objects: **Hoe kom ik bij het station?** 'How do I get to
the station?' **Ik kom vanavond bij je** 'I'll come over to your place tonight'.
Je moet bij de directeur komen 'You have to come to the director.'

Locations

This is a very large group of prepositions, and it is difficult to give examples for each possible situation. Some translate literally into their English

equivalent (an example is **achter** 'behind'), but others (such as **aan, bij, op**) are much more context dependent and don't translate literally. They have to be memorized.

aan	Often used to indicate that a person or object is literally alongside something, but also in more abstract meanings. **Ik zit aan tafel**. 'I'm sitting at the table.' **Karel studeert aan de universiteit**. 'Carl studies at the university.' **Het schip ligt aan wal.** 'The ship is on the shore.' **De mannen zijn nog aan boord.** 'The men are still on board.' **De was hangt aan de lijn.** 'The laundry is on the clothes line.'
achter	Always used to say that something is behind, literally or in an abstract way. **De schuur is achter het huis.** 'The shed is behind the house.' **Ik lig een week achter in mijn werk**. 'I'm a week behind in my work.'
beneden	Used to indicate that something is literally or figuratively beneath or below. **Beneden mij woont een pianist.** 'A pianist lives below me.' **Dat is toch beneden jouw niveau.** 'That's below your level, don't you think?'
bij	Indicates many different varieties of closeness, nearness. **Niels werkt bij de firma Giessen & Co.** 'Niels works at Giessen & Co.' **Ik heb die bloemen bij Van Dijk gekocht.** 'I bought those flowers at Van Dijk's.' **Jeroen woont bij z'n vriendin.** 'Jeroen lives with his girlfriend.' **Heb je geld bij je?** 'Do you have money with you?' **Is er een fietsenstalling bij het station?** 'Is there a bike storage at the station?' **Bij slecht weer vaart de pont niet.** 'The ferry doesn't run in bad weather.'
binnen	Used to say that something is within, referring to a place or to time. **Wil je wel binnen het hek blijven?** 'Please do stay within the fence, ok?' **U moet dit formulier binnen een week terugsturen.** 'You must send the form back within a week.'
boven	Means that something is literally or figuratively above. **Die foto hing vroeger boven mijn bed.** 'That photo used to hang above my bed.' **Dat is boven mijn budget.** 'That's above my spending level.'
buiten	Used to indicate that something is outside. **Hij woont buiten de stad.** 'He lives outside the city.' **Deze trein is buiten dienst.** 'This train is not in service.'
in	Refers to buildings, countries, cities, vehicles and other locations always meaning in or inside. **In de trein mag je niet meer roken.** 'You may no longer smoke in the train.' **Hij woont in Leiden.** 'He lives in Leiden.'

langs Always means alongside of something. **Er stonden veel oleanders langs de Italiaanse autowegen.** 'There were many oleanders along the Italian highways.'

naast Literally and figuratively next to. **Er woont een drugsdealer naast me.** 'A drug dealer lives next door to me.' **Naast mijn schoolwerk heb ik ook nog veel andere activiteiten.** 'Besides my school work I have a lot of other activities.' Note: English-speaking students of Dutch often confuse **naast** with 'next', as in 'next week'. That is **volgend**, so **volgende week**.

om Means that something is around something else. **De winkel is om de hoek.** 'The shop is around the corner.' **Hij heeft een dikke das om zijn nek.** 'He's got a thick scarf around his neck.'

onder Refers to something underneath something else, also in a figurative way. **Mijn bril ligt onder de krant.** 'My glasses are under the paper.' **Er werken driehonderd mensen onder mij.** 'Three hundred people work under me.'

op Refers to things that are literally on top of something. However, also used to say that one is actually in or at a certain place. **De vaas staat op de tafel.** 'The vase is on the table.' **Ik ben op school.** 'I am at school.' **Kees woont op kamers.** 'Kees lives on his own.' **Peter zit op voetbal.** 'Peter plays soccer.' **De koeien staan op stal.** 'The cows are in the stable.'

rond Used to say that something is around something else, often in combination with **om: rondom. De bestuursleden zaten rond de tafel.** 'The board members sat around the table.' **Er stonden oude huisjes rond (rondom) de kerk.** 'There were little old houses around the church.'

tegen Used to say that something is against, literally or more in an abstract way. **De fiets stond tegen het hek.** 'The bike was leaning against the fence.' **Hij is tegen dit voorstel.** He is against this proposal.

tegenover Something is opposite/across from something else. Also used for persons. **Tegenover mij woont een advocaat.** 'A lawyer lives across from me.' **De supermarkt is tegenover de bank.** 'The supermarket is opposite the bank.'

tussen Something is placed between two other things. Also used for persons. **Mijn huis staat tussen twee winkels.** 'My house is between two shops.' **Peter staat op deze foto tussen Erik en Sanne.** 'In this photo, Peter is between Erik and Sanne.'

voor As the opposite of **achter**, used to say that something is in front of something else. **De auto staat voor het huis.** 'The car is in front of the house.' Also used to express the opposite of **tegen**. **Ik ben voor jouw voorstel.** 'I support your proposal.'

Double prepositions

In a combination of two prepositions, one of the prepositions is placed before the noun or pronoun, and one after (postposition). First, some examples in context:

Op zijn fietstocht naar school fietst Peter eerst *onder* een viaduct *door*. Na vijf minuten moet hij *over* een smalle brug *heen*. Een beetje later fietst hij *om* een groot plein *heen*, daarna *tussen* twee hoge flatgebouwen *door* en tenslotte direct *op* het schoolgebouw *af*. En meestal fietst hij de hele weg *tegen* de wind *in*.
On his bike ride to school, Peter first goes under an overpass. After five minutes he has to cross a narrow bridge. A little later he bikes around a large square, then between two highrises and finally straight towards the school building. And most of the time, he has a head wind.

Some commonly used double prepositions

achter ... aan	Used to say that something or someone is following behind or going after something or someone. **De politie ging achter de dief aan.** 'The police went after the thief.' **Het stuk van Mozart komt achter het stuk van Strauss aan.** 'The piece by Mozart follows the piece by Strauss.'
door ... heen	All the way through. **Peter fietst door het park heen.** 'Peter bikes through the park.'
met ... mee	Going with. **Ik ga met je mee naar die film.** 'I'm going with you to that movie.' **Peter fietst met de wind mee.** 'Peter has a tail wind.'
naar ... toe	Towards. **Ik moet naar huis toe.** 'I have to go home.'
onder ... door	Under and through. **De boot vaart onder de brug door.** 'The boat is going underneath the bridge.'
op ... af	Going towards. **De hond kwam blaffend op mij af.** 'The barking dog came (running) towards me.'
over ... heen	(Getting) over. **Het paard sprong over de hindernis heen.** 'The horse jumped over the bar.' **Zij kwam niet over de dood van haar kind heen.** 'She couldn't get over the death of her child.'
tegen ... aan	Going, leaning against. **Het kind leunde tegen haar moeder aan.** 'The child leaned on her mother.' **Hij reed tegen een paal aan.** 'He drove into a pole.'
tussen ... door	In between. **Hij reed tussen twee flatgebouwen door.** 'He drove between two highrises.' **Tussen de lessen door gaan de studenten naar de kantine.** 'In between classes students go to the cafeteria.'

Prepositions expressing a reason or cause

Pre-
positions
express-
ing a
reason or
cause

door	through, because of	uit	out of
van	from	vanwege/wegens	because of

door
: Gives a reason or a cause. **Door de mist kon Erik niets op de weg zien.** 'Because of the fog, Erik couldn't see anything on the road.' **Door mijn onhandigheid is dat document op de verkeerde plaats gekomen.** 'Because of my clumsiness, that file landed in the wrong place.'

uit
: Used mostly for emotions. **Uit woede brak ze een kopje.** 'In her anger, she broke a cup.' **Uit jaloersheid zei hij die lelijke dingen.** 'He said those ugly things out of jealousy.'

van
: Gives a reason or cause, similar to **door. Hij ziet blauw van de kou.** 'He is freezing.' **Zij bloosde van schaamte.** 'She blushed with shame.' **Die auto is bruin van de roest.** 'That car is brown with rust.'

vanwege
: Gives a reason, as does **wegens. Vanwege de regen is de wedstrijd afgelast.** 'The match has been canceled because of the rain.' **De student werd wegens frequente absentie geschorst.** 'Because of frequent absences, the student was suspended.'

Other prepositions

possession
: The most commonly used prepositions for possession are **van** and **voor. Dat boek is van mij.** 'That book is mine.' **Voor wie is deze koffie?** 'For whom is this coffee?'

opinion
: To express an opinion, we use **volgens, voor** and **tegen. Volgens Peter is de film uitverkocht.** 'According to Peter, the movie is sold out.' **Ben jij voor of tegen kernraketten?** 'Are you for or against nuclear missiles?'

means
: For means or manner, we use **met** most of the time. **Erik gaat met de auto naar werk.** 'Erik takes the car to work.' **Ik moest die doos met een mes openmaken.** 'I had to open the box with a knife.'

two more
: Two more prepositions that we often see are **ondanks** 'despite' and **zonder** 'without'. **Ondanks de regen gingen we wandelen.** 'Despite the rain, we went for a hike.' **Zonder jas was het wel een beetje koud buiten.** 'Without a coat it was a little cold outside.'

Postpositions

A significant number of prepositions, when used in sentences expressing motion in a certain direction, are placed after the noun and are therefore called postpositions. In the group below, **af** is always a postposition. All of the others can be a preposition or a postposition, depending on the context.

af	down	**binnen**	into	**door**	through	**in**	into
langs	along	**om**	around	**op**	onto, up	**over**	over
rond	around	**uit**	out of, from	**voorbij**	past		

Examples:

De gast liep de trap *af* en het restaurant *binnen*.
The guest went *down* the stairs and *into* the restaurant.

Peter fietst het park *door* en rijdt een paar minuten later de stad *in*.
Peter bikes *through* the park and a few minutes later he rides *into* the city.

U gaat hier de gracht *langs* en bij de Rembrandtstraat moet u de hoek *om*.
You walk *along* the canal here, and at Rembrandtstraat you have to go *around* the corner.

De gast ging de trap *op* naar zijn kamer.
The guest went *up* the stairs to his room.

De bus met touristen reed de brug *over* en het plein *rond*.
The touringbus drove *over* the bridge and *around* the square.

De leerling die de klas *uit* was gestuurd liep snel het kantoor van de rector *voorbij*.
The student who had been sent *out of* the classroom quickly walked *past* the principal's office.

Exercise 25.1

Enter the correct prepositions in the sentences below the images.

1 De tas staat _____ de tafel.

2 De bloemen staan _____ de vaas.

3 De student zit _____ z'n buro.

4 De prullenbak staat _____ de tafel.

5 Het potlood ligt _____ het boek.

6 Het potlood ligt _____ het boek.

7 Het schilderij hangt _____ de tafel.

8 Het schilderij hangt _____ de ramen.

9 De stoel staat _____ de tafel.

10 De boom staat _____ het huis.

25
Pre-
positions

Exercise 25.2

Enter the correct preposition or postposition.

Situation: Asking for directions in the hospital.

Meneer A: Pardon, ik moet _____ (1) de röntgenafdeling. Hoe kom ik daar?
Receptionist: A ja, u gaat hier rechtdoor _____ (2) de trap. U gaat de trap _____ (3) naar de tweede verdieping. Of u gaat _____ (4) de lift, dat kan ook. Daar gaat u _____ (5) links en u loopt steeds maar rechtdoor _____ (6) het eind van de gang. Daar weer links en dan loopt u _____ (7) de verpleegsterskamer en de toiletten _____ (8) de röntgenkamer. U moet even uw naam _____ (9) de receptioniste opgeven en u kunt _____ (10) de wachtkamer gaan zitten. U wordt dan opgeroepen.

Exercise 25.3

Enter the correct preposition of time.

1 Erik is _____ mei jarig, maar ik weet niet precies _____ welke datum.
2 Karin heeft _____ maandagmorgen _____ half negen wiskunde.
3 _____ 12.00 en 1.00 uur is deze winkel voor de lunch gesloten.
4 _____ het eten staat de televisie bij ons nooit aan.
5 A: Hoe laat komt de trein? B: Ik denk _____ tien minuten.
6 Deze bus rijdt elk half uur, om kwart _____ en kwart _____.
7 A: Hoe laat kom je vanavond? B: Ik weet het niet precies, _____ acht uur?
8 A: Hoe vaak sport jij? B: Twee keer _____ week, _____ maandag en donderdag.
9 _____ 2006 zijn we in Indonesië op vakantie geweest.
10 Peters voetbaltraining duurt _____ 7.00 uur _____ 9.00 uur.

Exercise 25.4

Use the correct double preposition: **op ... af, door ... heen, naar ... toe, onder ... door, met ... mee, tegen ... aan, tussen ... door, achter ... aan.**

1 Peter en Karin fietsen _____ het bevroren kanaal _____ om te schaatsen.
2 Bij het kanaal zetten ze hun fietsen _____ een hek _____.
3 Ze schaatsen eerst naar het zuiden, lekker _____ de wind _____.
4 Peter schaatst voorop en Karin schaatst _____ Peter _____.

5 In de dorpjes schaatsen ze _____ veel bruggen _____.
6 Maar na een half uur schaatst Peter recht _____ een zwakke plek in het ijs _____ .
7 Hij ziet het te laat en zakt tot zijn middel _____ het ijs _____.
8 Karin helpt hem eruit en samen klimmen ze op de wal. Gelukkig zijn ze dichtbij een dorp en zo lopen ze, Peter helemaal nat, _____ verbaasde mensen _____ naar een warm café.

Exercise 25.5

In the sentences with the images, enter the correct postposition.

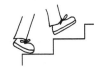

1 Hij gaat de trap _____.

2 Hij gaat de trap _____.

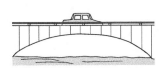

3 De auto gaat de brug _____.

4 Erik komt het café _____.

5 Erik loopt de gracht _____.

6 Erik loopt het huis _____.

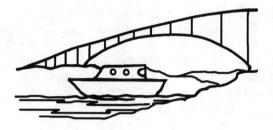

De boot vaart onder de brug door.

APPENDIX
Strong and irregular verbs

Introduction

The following is a list of commonly used strong and irregular verbs. The strong verbs are organized according to the way they change their stem vowel in the simple past and the present perfect tense. This is an easier way for students to recognize and memorize patterns than if they were listed in alphabetical order.

a – oe – a

dragen	**droeg**	**gedragen**	carry, wear
ervaren	**ervoer**	**ervaren**	experience
graven	**groef**	**gegraven**	dig
slaan	**sloeg**	**geslagen**	hit, strike
varen	**voer**	**gevaren**	float, sail

a – ie/i – a

bevallen	**beviel**	**bevallen**	please, give birth
blazen	**blies**	**geblazen**	blow
laten	**liet**	**gelaten**	let
slapen	**sliep**	**geslapen**	sleep
vallen	**viel**	**gevallen**	fall
hangen	**hing**	**gehangen**	hang
vangen	**ving**	**gevangen**	catch

e – a – e

eten	**at**	**gegeten**	eat
genezen	**genas**	**genezen**	heal
geven	**gaf**	**gegeven**	give
lezen	**las**	**gelezen**	read

meten	mat	gemeten	measure
treden	trad	getreden	step, move
vergeten	vergat	vergeten	forget
vreten	vrat	gevreten	devour, gobble

e – a – o

bevelen	beval	bevolen	order, command
breken	brak	gebroken	break
nemen	nam	genomen	take
spreken	sprak	gesproken	speak
steken	stak	gestoken	stick, sting, prick
stelen	stal	gestolen	steal

e – ie – a

| scheppen | schiep | geschapen | create |

e – ie – e

| heffen | hief | geheven | lift, heave |

e – ie – o

bederven	bedierf	bedorven	spoil, rot
helpen	hielp	geholpen	help
ontwerpen	ontwierp	ontworpen	design
sterven	stierf	gestorven	die
werpen	wierp	geworpen	throw
werven	wierf	geworven	recruit
zwerven	zwierf	gezworven	wander, roam

e – o – o

bedelven	bedolf	bedolven	overwhelm, bury
bergen	borg	geborgen	store, save
bewegen	bewoog	bewogen	move
delven	dolf	gedolven	dig, unearth
gelden	gold	gegolden	apply, count
melken	molk	gemolken	milk
schelden	schold	gescholden	scoff, scold
schenden	schond	geschonden	violate
schenken	schonk	geschonken	give, donate
scheren	schoor	geschoren	shave

smelten	smolt	gesmolten	melt
treffen	trof	getroffen	meet, strike
trekken	trok	getrokken	pull
vechten	vocht	gevochten	fight
vertrekken	vertrok	vertrokken	depart
vlechten	vlocht	gevlochten	braid, twine
wegen	woog	gewogen	weigh
zenden	zond	gezonden	send
zwellen	zwol	gezwollen	swell
zwemmen	zwom	gezwommen	swim

e – oe – o

zweren	zwoer	gezworen	swear

i – a – e

bidden	bad	gebeden	pray
liggen	lag	gelegen	lie (down)
zitten	zat	gezeten	sit

i – o – o

beginnen	begon	begonnen	begin
bezinnen (zich)	bezon	bezonnen	ponder
binden	bond	gebonden	bind
blinken	blonk	geblonken	gleam, glitter
dingen	dong	gedongen	haggle, bargain
dringen	drong	gedrongen	push forward
drinken	dronk	gedronken	drink
dwingen	dwong	gedwongen	force
glimmen	glom	geglommen	shine, gleam
klimmen	klom	geklommen	climb
klinken	klonk	geklonken	sound, hammer
krimpen	kromp	gekrompen	shrink
opwinden	wond op	opgewonden	wind up, excite
schrikken	schrok	geschrokken	be scared, startled
slinken	slonk	geslonken	decrease
spinnen	spon	gesponnen	spin, purr
springen	sprong	gesprongen	jump, spring
stinken	stonk	gestonken	stink
verzinnen	verzon	verzonnen	contrive, make up

vinden	vond	gevonden	find
winden	wond	gewonden	wind
winnen	won	gewonnen	win
wringen	wrong	gewrongen	wrench, wring out
zingen	zong	gezongen	sing
zinken	zonk	gezonken	sink

ie – oo – o

bedriegen	bedroog	bedrogen	cheat
bieden	bood	geboden	offer
gieten	goot	gegoten	pour
kiezen	koos	gekozen	choose
liegen	loog	gelogen	lie
opschieten	schoot op	opgeschoten	hurry up
schieten	schoot	geschoten	shoot
verbieden	verbood	verboden	forbid
verliezen	verloor	verloren	lose
vliegen	vloog	gevlogen	fly
vriezen	vroor	gevroren	freeze

ij – ee – e

begrijpen	begreep	begrepen	understand
bijten	beet	gebeten	bite
blijken	bleek	gebleken	appear
blijven	bleef	gebleven	stay
drijven	dreef	gedreven	float, drive (push)
glijden	gleed	gegleden	slide, glide
grijpen	greep	gegrepen	seize, grab
hijsen	hees	gehesen	raise, hoist
kijken	keek	gekeken	look
knijpen	kneep	geknepen	pinch
krijgen	kreeg	gekregen	get, receive
lijden	leed	geleden	suffer
lijken	leek	geleken	appear
mijden	meed	gemeden	avoid, shun
overlijden	overleed	overleden	pass away
prijzen	prees	geprezen	praise, price
rijden	reed	gereden	drive
rijgen	reeg	geregen	tie, string
rijzen	rees	gerezen	rise

schijnen	scheen	geschenen	shine, appear
schrijven	schreef	geschreven	write
slijpen	sleep	geslepen	sharpen
slijten	sleet	gesleten	wear out, spend, sell
smijten	smeet	gesmeten	throw, toss
snijden	sneed	gesneden	cut
spijten	speet	gespeten	regret, be sorry
splijten	spleet	gespleten	split, crack
stijgen	steeg	gestegen	rise, increase
strijden	streed	gestreden	fight, struggle
strijken	streek	gestreken	iron, brush
verdwijnen	verdween	verdwenen	disappear
vergelijken	vergeleek	vergeleken	compare
verwijten	verweet	verweten	blame
wijken	week	geweken	make way for
wijzen	wees	gewezen	point
wrijven	wreef	gewreven	rub, buff
zwijgen	zweeg	gezwegen	be silent

ui – oo – o

buigen	boog	gebogen	bend, bow
druipen	droop	gedropen	drip
duiken	dook	gedoken	dive
fluiten	floot	gefloten	whistle
kluiven	kloof	gekloven	nibble, gnaw
kruipen	kroop	gekropen	crawl
ruiken	rook	geroken	smell
schuiven	schoof	geschoven	push, shove
sluipen	sloop	geslopen	sneak, creep
sluiten	sloot	gesloten	close, lock
snuiten	snoot	gesnoten	blow nose, snuff
snuiven	snoof	gesnoven	sniff, snort
spuiten	spoot	gespoten	spout, gush, inject
stuiven	stoof	gestoven	blow, dust
verschuilen	verschool	verscholen	hide
zuigen	zoog	gezogen	suck
zuipen	zoop	gezopen	drink, booze

The following is a list of strong verbs that don't seem to follow a clear pattern such as the ones above or are alone in their pattern. They are organized here in alphabetical order.

doen	deed	gedaan	do
gaan	ging	gegaan	go
houden	hield	gehouden	hold
komen	kwam	gekomen	come
lopen	liep	gelopen	walk
roepen	riep	geroepen	call
staan	stond	gestaan	stand
weten	wist	geweten	know
worden	werd	geworden	become
zien	zag	gezien	see

The following is a list of irregular verbs. They are irregular because one of their past tense forms is strong, and one is regular, or their past tense forms seem to follow the rules for regular verbs. They are organized in alphabetical order.

bakken	bakte	gebakken	bake
barsten	barstte	gebarsten	burst
bezoeken	bezocht	bezocht	visit
braden	braadde	gebraden	fry, sauté
brengen	bracht	gebracht	bring
denken	dacht	gedacht	think
hebben	had	gehad	have
heten	heette	geheten	be called
jagen	joeg	gejaagd	hunt
kopen	kocht	gekocht	buy
lachen	lachte	gelachen	laugh
laden	laadde	geladen	load
malen	maalde	gemalen	grind, ground
raden	raadde	geraden	guess
scheiden	scheidde	gescheiden	separate
spannen	spande	gespannen	stretch, tighten
stoten	stootte	gestoten	bump, knock
verraden	verraadde	verraden	cheat, betray
vouwen	vouwde	gevouwen	fold
vragen	vroeg	gevraagd	ask
waaien	woei/waaide	gewaaid	blow
wassen	waste	gewassen	wash
weven	weefde	geweven	weave
zeggen	zei, zeiden	gezegd	say
zijn	was, waren	geweest	be
zoeken	zocht	gezocht	look for
zouten	zoutte	gezouten	salt, pickle

KEY TO EXERCISES

Unit 1

Exercise 1.1

a wij/we. b ik. c u. d jullie. e u. f jij/je. g zij/ze. h hij, zij/ze, het.

Exercise 1.2

1 ik. 2 hij. 3 hij. 4 zij/ze. 5 ze. 6 hij. 7 We. 8 zij/ze. 9 Zij/Ze. 10 We. 11 jullie.

Exercise 1.3

1 je. 2 Ik, jij. 3 Ik, je. 4 Ik. 5 je. 6 Hij, jij. 7 Ik, Zij/Ze. 8 we.

Exercise 1.4

1 u. 2 we. 3 jij/je. 4 u. 5 wij/we, jullie. 6 Ze. 7 ik. 8 Ze, je.

Exercise 1.5

1 Hij. 2 Ze. 3 Ik. 4 Hij. 5 Ze. 6 Het. 7 We. 8 Hij.

Exercise 1.6

1 vraag, vragen. 2 zeg, zeggen. 3 neem, nemen. 4 zwem, zwemmen. 5 leef, leven. 6 reis, reizen. 7 heb, hebben. 8 loop, lopen. 9 zit, zitten. 10 laat, laten.

Exercise 1.7

1 koop, koopt, koop je, koopt, kopen, kopen, kopen. 2 pas, past, pas je, past, passen, passen, passen. 3 eet, eet, eet je, eet, eten, eten, eten. 4 schrijf, schrijft, schrijf je, schrijft, schrijven, schrijven, schrijven. 5 lees, leest, lees je, leest, lezen, lezen, lezen.

Exercise 1.8

1 Ga. 2 Koop. 3 Drink. 4 Bezoek. 5 Eet.

Exercise 1.9

1 ben. 2 is. 3 heb. 4 is. 5 is. 6 hebben. 7 heeft. 8 heb. 9 heeft. 10 zijn.
11 is. 12 Heb.

Exercise 1.10

1 is. 2 spel. 3 kom. 4 woon. 5 studeer. 6 werk. 7 heet. 8 werkt. 9 woont.
10 komt. 11 gaan. 12 ben. 13 Kom. 14 woon. 15 ben. 16 ben.

Exercise 1.11

1 is. 2 koopt. 3 vraagt. 4 neemt. 5 betaalt. 6 heeft. 7 gaat. 8 zegt. 9 weegt.
10 vindt. 11 snijdt. 12 is.

Unit 2

Exercise 2.1

1 Erik, *wil* je het vuilnis buitenzetten? 2 Ja, dat *zal* ik doen. 3 *Kun* je
de stofzuiger even boven brengen? 4 *Zullen* we eerst koffie drinken?
5 Goed, *wil* jij dan even koffie zetten? 6 Hè, ik *moet* hier altijd alles
doen!

Exercise 2.2

1 Mogen. 2 Kunt. 3 Wilt. 4 Mag. 5 zullen. 6 wil. 7 kunt. 8 mag. 9 zal. 10
wil.

Exercise 2.3

Speaking exercise. Check answers with instructor.

Unit 3

Exercise 3.1

1 Hoe gaat het op school? 2 Wie is je beste vriendin? 3 Wanneer begint
de zomervakantie? 4 Wat wil je eten? 5 Waarom eet je zo weinig?

Exercise 3.2

1 Wat. 2 Waar. 3 welke. 4 welk. 5 Wanneer. 6 Hoe laat. 7 Hoe. 8 Hoe.

Exercise 3.3

1 Wat. 2 Welke. 3 Welke/Wat voor. 4 Hoe. waar. 5 Hoe.

Exercise 3.4

1 Hoe. 2 Hoeveel. 3 Wat/Hoeveel. 4 Welke. 5 Waar ... vandaan. 6 Hoe. 7 Wat/Hoeveel. 8 Wanneer. 9 Welke. 10 Hoeveel.

Exercise 3.5

1 Hoe heet je/Wat is je naam? 2 Wat is je achternaam? 3 Waar kom je vandaan? 4 Wat studeer je? 5 Wat wil je drinken?

Exercise 3.6

1 Hoe groot is de kamer? 2 Is de kamer gemeubileerd?/Heeft de kamer meubels? 3 Heeft de kamer een balkon? 4 Met hoeveel personen moet ik de keuken en de badkamer delen? 5 Mag ik huisdieren hebben? 6 Wat/Hoeveel/Hoe hoog is de huur? 7 Wanneer kan ik de kamer bekijken? 8 Ja, hoe laat? 9 Wat is het adres? 10 O, mag ik in de kamer roken?

Exercise 3.7

1 Hoe laat vertrekt de trein naar Groningen? 2 Van welk spoor vertrekt de trein? 3 Wat kost een enkele reis naar Groningen? 4 Waar kan ik hier iets eten? 5 Hoe kom ik van het station in Groningen naar het centrum? 6 Welke bus rijdt naar het centrum? 7 Hoeveel strippen heb ik nodig? 8 Hoe lang duurt de rit van het station naar het centrum?

Unit 4

Exercise 4.1

a drie. b elf. c veertien. d vijfendertig. e tweehonderdzevenenzestig. f achthonderdvierennegentig. g duizend zeven. h vijftienhonderdtachtig/ duizend vijfhonderdtachtig. i tweeduizend driehonderdzesenvijftig/ drieëntwintighonderdzesenvijftig. j negentienhonderdtweeënzestig/ duizend negenhonderdtweeënzestig. k vierduizend twintig. l vijfenveertigduizend zeshonderdzevenentwintig.

Exercise 4.2

1 eenentwintig mei negentien(honderd)drieëntachtig. 2 drie december
tweeduizend zes. 3 negen september negentien(honderd)negenennegentig.
4 zes januari negentien(honderd)vijfenzeventig. 5 twaalf maart tweeduizend twee.

Exercise 4.3

1 de twaalfde september. 2 de negende oktober. 3 de dertigste april. 4 de
veertiende juni. 5 de zesentwintigste december.

Exercise 4.4

1 drie. 2 zestien vierkante meter. 3 vijftien juli. 4 één meter tweeënnegentig.
5 tweeëntachtig kilo. 6 dertien kilometer. 7 tien euro tachtig. 8 vierhon-
derdnegenentachtig euro. 9 achtste. 10 vijfde.

Exercise 4.5

1 vijf kilo. 2 anderhalf pond. 3 twee liter. 4 honderd gram. 5 een half.

Exercise 4.6

1 kilo. 2 kilometer. 3 liters. 4 pond. 5 kilo.

Exercise 4.7

1 eerste. 2 tweede. 3 twintig. 4 derde. 5 vier. 6 veertigste. 7 honderd.
8 vijftigste. 9 tien. 10 achtste.

Unit 5

Exercise 5.1

1 tien over drie. 2 kwart voor twaalf. 3 vijf voor half zeven. 4 vijf voor
negen. 5 vijf over half één.

Exercise 5.2

1 Erik wordt om zeven uur wakker. 2 Erik zit om kwart over tien in een
vergadering.

Exercise 5.3

1 Sanne speelt op donderdagavond tennis. 2 Mieke en Hans komen op zaterdagavond. 3 Sanne gaat op vrijdagmiddag naar de Amnesty-groep. 4 Sanne werkt op vrijdag niet. 5 Ze drinkt op vrijdagochtend/morgen koffie met Sara. 6 Sanne gaat om acht uur naar de film. 7 Ze moet om kwart over twee naar dokter Meijer. 8 Karin moet om tien over drie naar de tandarts. 9 De computerles is om kwart voor vier. 10 De schoolvergadering is om half acht.

Exercise 5.4

1 laat. 2 straks. 3 binnenkort. 4 toen. 5 al. 6 Nu. 7 ooit. 8 net. 9 vroeg. 10 pas.

Exercise 5.5

Speaking exercise. Check answers with instructor.

Unit 6

Exercise 6.1

1 definite. 2 indefinite. 3 indefinite. 4 definite. 5 indefinite.

Exercise 6.2

1 een. 2 De. 3 de. 4 –. 5 –. 6 –. 7 de. 8 een. 9 een. 10 –. 11 een. 12 een. 13 de. 14 het. 15 De. 16 het. 17 de. 18 De. 19 een. 20 een.

Exercise 6.3

1 het toiletpapier. 2 de pindakaas. 3 de koffiemelk. 4 de boterkoek. 5 het wasmiddel. 6 de poedersuiker. 7 de tandpasta. 8 de chocoladevla. 9 het soepvlees. 10 de aardappelsalade. 11 de handcrème. 12 het bronwater.

Exercise 6.4

A 1 –. 2 een. 3 –. 4 een. 5 een. 6 Het. 7 de. 8 –. 9 een. 10 een.
B 1 –. 2 de. 3 –. 4 een. 5 een. 6 een. 7 een. 8 een. 9 een. 10 een.
C 1 de. 2 een. 3 Het. 4 –. 5 De. 6 de. 7 het. 8 het. 9 de. 10 het.

Unit 7

Exercise 7.1

huizen, jaren, straten, auto's, winkels, supermarkten, kinderen, parken, bomen, bioscopen, restaurants, tennisbanen, voetbalvelden.

Exercise 7.2

1 tomaten. 2 druiven. 3 zakken. 4 aubergines. 5 meloenen. 6 potten. 7 bekers. 8 bonen.

Exercise 7.3

1 verdiepingen. 2 slaapkamers. 3 banken. 4 kussens. 5 bijzettafeltjes. 6 gordijnen. 7 ramen. 8 lampen. 9 stoelen. 10 vloerkleden. 11 boekenkasten.

Exercise 7.4

1 bedden. 2 lakens. 3 vloeren. 4 toiletten. 5 boodschappen. 6 vuilnisbakken. 7 aardappels/aardappelen. 8 kattenbakken. 9 honden. 10 flessen.

Exercise 7.5

1 kopjes. 2 glazen. 3 sigaretten. 4 zakken. 5 eieren. 6 koekjes. 7 gehaktballen. 8 pinda's. 9 appels. 10 bananen.

Unit 8

Exercise 8.1

1 het. 2 hem. 3 ze. 4 hem. 5 haar. 6 het. 7 hem. 8 hen. 9 ons. 10 jullie.

Exercise 8.2

1 mij. 2 u, me. 3 je. 4 ons. 5 hen/ze. 6 ze. 7 jullie. 8 jou. 9 hem. 10 haar.

Exercise 8.3

1 hem. 2 haar. 3 haar, ze. 4 mij. 5 hen.

Exercise 8.4

1 hem. 2 het. 3 ze. 4 ze. 5 hem. 6 hem. 7 hen/ze. 8 me.

Exercise 8.5

1 jullie. 2 ik. 3 Ik, jij. 4 me. 5 u, het. 6 hem, haar. 7 mij. 8 ik. 9 u. 10 ons.
11 hij. 12 we. 13 mij/me. 14 mij. 15 jou, mij.

Unit 9

Exercise 9.1

1 dit. 2 deze. 3 die. 4 die. 5 dat. 6 deze. 7 die. 8 deze. 9 die. 10 Dit.

Exercise 9.2

1 fout. 2 fout. 3 goed. 4 goed. 5 goed.

Exercise 9.3

1 Die. 2 dat. 3 die. 4 Die. 5 dat.

Exercise 9.4

1 deze, die. 2 die, dat. 3 dit, dat, dat. 4 dat, deze. 5 die, dit.

Unit 10

Exercise 10.1

Possessive pronouns: mijn, m'n, onze, mijn, hun, Mijn, zijn, mijn, haar, haar,
hun, z'n, Hun, d'r, onze.

Exercise 10.2

1 je. 2 haar/d'r. 3 zijn/z'n. 4 haar/d'r. 5 jullie. 6 hun. 7 mijn/m'n. 8 je.

Exercise 10.3

1 je. 2 Mijn/M'n. 3 mijn/m'n. 4 onze. 5 hun, jullie.

Exercise 10.4

1 Mijn/M'n. 2 Haar. 3 Hun. 4 hun. 5 Onze. 6 zijn/z'n. 7 mijn/m'n.
8 zijn/z'n.

Exercise 10.5

1 ik. 2 u. 3 mijn/m'n. 4 Uw. 5 onze, We. 6 uw. 7 jij/je. 8 me. 9 mijn/m'n.
10 ik, u.

Unit 11

Exercise 11.1

Predicate adjectives: lang, duur, goedkoop, zwaar.

Exercise 11.2

Attributive adjectives: grote, verse, Mooie, rode, nieuwe, middelgrote, grote.

Exercise 11.3

1 witte, gekookte, zwarte. 2 koude, verse. 3 gebakken. 4 Zaanse, wit,
bruin. 5 Wit, bruin, jonge, oude. 6 gerookte. 7 Gestoofde, witte. 8 Warm.
9 Eigengemaakt, warme. 10 Griekse, vers.

Exercise 11.4

1 Jonge. 2 zoute. 3 Mager. 4 diverse. 5 halve. 6 Bruin. 7 Witte. 8 groot.
9 volle. 10 Verse.

Exercise 11.5

1 groot. 2 mooie. 3 ruime. 4 grote. 5 groot. 6 moderne. 7 kleine. 8 leren.
9 antieke. 10 zilveren. 11 dure. 12 hoge. 13 zwart. 14 oude. 15 nieuwe.

Unit 12

Exercise 12.1

1 beter. 2 sterkere. 3 meer. 4 zoeter. 5 vetter. 6 groter. 7 leukere. 8 lekkerder. 9 zachter. 10 liever.

Exercise 12.2

1 grootste. 2 langste. 3 hoogste. 4 oudste. 5 meeste. 6 beste. 7 lekkerste.
8 populairste. 9 snelste. 10 sympathiekste.

Exercise 12.3

1 mooiste. 2 kleine. 3 groter. 4 meer. 5 leukste. 6 stomme. 7 lange. 8 mooiste.
9 dikker. 10 meeste.

Exercise 12.4

1 kleiner, groter, minst, meer. 2 grootst, minder, meer, vaakst/meest,
oudste. 3 jonger, kleinste, meest/vaakst, minder, kortst, meer. 4 jongste,
meeste, minder, meeste, meest/langst, minder, verst.

Unit 13

Exercise 13.1

1 heel. 2 graag, dadelijk. 3 eigenlijk, Vanmiddag, toch. 4 mooi, vreselijk.
5 even, nu, echt.

Exercise 13.2

1 adverb. 2 adverb. 3 adjective. 4 adverb. 5 adjective.

Exercise 13.3

1 Erik wil zaterdag naar de voetbalwedstrijd. 2 De kaarten voor de voetbalwedstrijd zijn compleet uitverkocht. 3 Erik vindt het heel jammer.
Hij wil de wedstrijd graag zien. 4 "Ik bestel meteen kaarten voor volgende week," zegt Erik. 5 "Sorry, meneer, maar die wedstrijd is ook
uitverkocht."

Exercise 13.4

1 Straks gaat Sanne naar de yogales. 2 Misschien gaat ze na de yogales
met Hester koffiedrinken. 3 Hopelijk heeft Hester tijd. 4 Gelukkig is het
mooi weer. 5 Dan kunnen ze buiten op een terras zitten.

Exercise 13.5

1 eindelijk. 2 net. 3 al. 4 vrij. 5 heel/hartstikke. 6 ook. 7 bijna. 8 helaas.
9 misschien. 10 heel/hartstikke.

Unit 14

Exercise 14.1

1 Hardegarijp. 2 tennisrackets. 3 yogales. 4 koeken. 5 een grote achtertuin.

Exercise 14.2

1 Er is een nieuwe kraam op de markt. 2 Je kunt er allerlei soorten brood kopen. 3 Sanne koopt er altijd harde broodjes. 4 Er staat een leuke verkoper in de kraam. 5a Sanne betaalt voor acht broodjes. 5b maar zij krijgt er tien.

Exercise 14.3

1 Hij drinkt er vier. 2 Hij eet er geen. 3 Hij doet er twee op zijn brood. 4 Hij eet er zes. 5 Hij drinkt er veel.

Exercise 14.4

1 Zit er vlees in de soep? 2 Zitten er champignons in de saus? 3 Wat zit er op de pizza? 4 Is er geen lasagne meer? 5 Zijn er geen asbakken?

Exercise 14.5

Speaking exercise. Check answers with instructor.

Unit 15

Exercise 15.1

1 fout. 2 fout. 3 goed. 4 goed. 5 fout.

Exercise 15.2

1 niet. 2 geen. 3 niet. 4 niet. 5 geen.

Exercise 15.3

1 niet. 2 geen. 3 niet. 4 geen. 5 niet. 6 geen.

Exercise 15.4

1 ✓ met de receptionist. 2 van Erik ✓. 3 ✓ voor beginners. 4 ✓ op maandag en woensdag. 5 ✓ doen. 6 ✓ dit semester. 7 ✓ duur. 8 ✓ met creditcard.

Exercise 15.5

1 Sanne is niet op de markt. 2 Zij heeft geen aardappels nodig. 3 Er zijn geen nieuwe aardappels. 4 De aardappels zijn niet duur. 5 Ze koopt deze week niet veel aardappels.

Exercise 15.6

1 Vandaag zijn Erik en Sanne niet in een restaurant. 2 Er zitten niet veel mensen in het restaurant. 3 De ober brengt de menukaart niet snel. 4 Erik neemt de soep van de dag niet. 5 Sanne wil de soep van de dag ook niet bestellen.

Exercise 15.7

1 Nee, dat is mijn rok niet. 2 Nee pap, ik heb geen blauwe onderbroek. 3 Nee Erik, die spijkerbroek is niet van Sem. 4 Nee oom Erik, dat zijn onze handdoeken niet. 5 Nee, die tennissokken zijn niet van mij.

Exercise 15.8

1 Nee, er is nog geen koffie. 2 Nee, de krant is er nog niet. 3 Nee, de kinderen zijn nog niet wakker. 4 Nee, de hond is nog niet uitgelaten. 5 Nee, er is nog geen post.

Exercise 15.9

1 Nee, er is geen soep meer. 2 Nee, ik heb geen kroketten meer. 3 Nee, de koffie is niet meer warm. 4 Nee, de keuken is niet meer open. 5 Nee, de chef is er niet meer.

Exercise 15.10

1 Nee, ik wil geen spa, maar ik wil wel appelsap. 2 Nee, ik ga niet naar de film, maar ik ga wel naar de disco. 3 Nee, ik wil geen peper, maar ik wil wel extra champignons. 4 Nee, we gaan niet naar Engeland, maar we gaan wel naar Frankrijk. 5 Nee, ik vind Brad Pitt geen goed acteur, maar ik vind George Clooney wel een goed acteur.

Unit 16

Exercise 16.1

1 kuikentjes – kuiken. 2 aapje – aap, stokje – stok. 3 hoedje – hoed. 4 paardje
– paard. 5 stationnetje – station. 6 parapluutje – paraplu, parasolletje –
parasol. 7 wagentje – wagen. 8 emmertjes – emmer. 9 kringetje – kring.
10 zakdoekje – zakdoek.

Exercise 16.2

1 kopje. 2 lepeltje. 3 plakjes. 4 glaasje. 5 schijfje. 6 bekertje. 7 stukje. 8
bordje. 9 flesje. 10 schaaltje.

Exercise 16.3

1 huisje. 2 autootje. 3 tuintje. 4 bloempjes/bloemetjes. 5 bedje. 6 glaasje.
7 broodje. 8 fietsje. 9 burootje/bureautje. 10 stoeltje. 11 papiertje. 12 pan-
netje. 13 fornuisje. 14 keukentje. 15 bordje. 16 teeveetje/televisietje.

Exercise 16.4

1 hondje. 2 tuintje, woninkje. 3 parkje. 4 balletje. 5 boompje. 6 parapluutje. 7 jasje. 8 eekhoorntjes. 9 pootjes. 10 eikeltjes.

Exercise 16.5

1 dingetjes. 2 jurkje. 3 sokjes. 4 truitje. 5 dekentje. 6 speelgoedje. 7 stukje.
8 wijntje. 9 nootjes. 10 zakje. 11 kilootje. 12 avondje.

Exercise 16.6

1 dutje. 2 ommetje. 3 hapje. 4 praatje. 5 biertje.

Unit 17

Exercise 17.1

1 Ja, ik ruim nu mijn kamer op. 2 Okee, ik bel oma op. 3 Goed, ik haal
de pizza op. 4 Jaha, ik trek mijn jas aan. 5 Nee, ik maak mijn huiswerk
niet af! 6 Nee, ik blijf vanavond niet thuis!

Exercise 17.2

Separable: aankomen, afspreken, uitgeven, instappen, aankleden, uittrekken, doorwerken, meewerken, langskomen, thuisblijven, tegenwerken, aanbieden, opnemen.
Inseparable: bespreken, geloven, vertrekken, ontwerpen, herkennen, bewerken, verfilmen, verbieden, ontnemen.

Exercise 17.3

1 stilstaan. 2 hardlopen. 3 goedkeuren. 4 kwijtraken. 5 grootbrengen.

Exercise 17.4

1 Erik heeft een zakenvriend ontmoet. 2 Sanne heeft oma Beumer opgebeld. 3 Peter is met een vriend uitgegaan. 4 Karin heeft lang uitgeslapen. 5 Erik heeft zijn paraplu vergeten. 6 Sanne heeft de meubels afgestoft. 7 Karin is met een breiwerk begonnen. 8 Peter heeft de vriend voor het eten uitgenodigd.

Unit 18

Exercise 18.1

1 d. 2 d. 3 t. 4 d. 5 d. 6 t. 7 d. 8 t. 9 t. 10 d. 11 d. 12 d. 13 t. 14 d. 15 t.

Exercise 18.2

1 heb. 2 heb. 3 ben. 4 heb. 5 ben. 6 heb. 7 heb. 8 ben. 9 heb. 10 ben.

Exercise 18.3

1 heb. 2 zijn. 3 hebben. 4 zijn, hebben. 5 zijn. 6 hebben, hebben. 7 zijn, heeft.

Exercise 18.4

1 geschoten. 2 gekregen. 3 gestonken. 4 gesloten. 5 gesproken.

Exercise 18.5

1 gedaan. 2 geluisterd. 3 geleerd. 4 gemaild. 5 gekeken. 6 gezien. 7 geweest. 8 gemaakt. 9 gelezen. 10 begonnen.

Exercise 18.6

1 Linda is met de tram naar het centrum gegaan. 2 Ze heeft bij de Bijenkorf een nieuwe jurk uitgezocht. 3 Ze heeft de jurk in de paskamer aangetrokken. 4 Ze heeft de jurk met creditcard betaald. 5 Een dag later heeft ze de jurk teruggebracht.

Unit 19

Exercise 19.1

1 te. 2 de. 3 de. 4 te. 5 de. 6 de. 7 te. 8 de. 9 te. 10 de. 11 te. 12 de. 13 de. 14 te. 15 de.

Exercise 19.2

brak (breken), ging (gaan), opende (openen), stal (stelen), zag (zien), waarschuwde (waarschuwen), arriveerde (arriveren), was (zijn), functioneerde (functioneren), beweerde (beweren), werkte (werken).

Exercise 19.3

1 gingen. 2 kampeerden. 3 aten. 4 zwommen. 5 wandelden. 6 zaten. 7 praatten. 8 was. 9 had. 10 blafte.

Exercise 19.4

1 Wij moesten altijd in het huishouden helpen. 2 Wij mochten 's avonds nooit lang buiten spelen. 3 Oma kon ons maar heel weinig zakgeld geven. 4 Opa wilde ons niet met ons huiswerk helpen. 5 Wij konden nooit op vakantie gaan.

Exercise 19.5

1 bekeek. 2 lag. 3 stond. 4 liet. 5 had. 6 zag. 7 was. 8 vond. 9 mocht. 10 nam.

Exercise 19.6

1 zat. 2 wachtte. 3 kwam. 4 ging. 5 bestelde. 6 stak . . . op. 7 zei. 8 mocht. 9 vroeg. 10 werd. 11 gooide. 12 was. 13 reden. 14 leende. 15 hing.

Unit 20

Exercise 20.1

1 geef. 2 doe. 3 kijk. 4 zeg. 5 vraag. 6 lees. 7 loop. 8 wees. 9 pak. 10 neem.
11 wacht. 12 schrijf.

Exercise 20.2

1 haal. 2 Doe. 3 breng. 4 geef. 5 zet.

Exercise 20.3

1 Schil. 2 Kook. 3 Snijd. 4 Open. 5 Doe. 6 Meng. 7 Giet. 8 Roer. 9 Zet.
10 Serveer.

Exercise 20.4

1 schiet op in de douche. 2 zet het ontbijt klaar. 3 laat even de hond uit.
4 doe deze envelop even op de bus. 5 neem je voetbalspullen mee. 6 vergeet
je lunch niet. 7 maak deze jampot even open. 8 doe je mobiele telefoon
uit. 9 geef me de boter even aan. 10 wees om zes uur thuis.

Exercise 20.5

1 Zegt. 2 Brengt. 3 Geeft. 4 neem. 5 geef. 6 Ga. 7 Vraag. 8 koop. 9 kom.
10 Zeur.

Unit 21

Exercise 21.1

1 je. 2 me. 3 ons. 4 zich. 5 je.

Exercise 21.2

1 Erik wast zich. 2 Erik scheert zich.

Exercise 21.3

1 me ... voorstellen. 2 Amuseert ... zich. 3 verheugen ons. 4 Vervelen ...
je. 5 voelt zich. 6 Verbaas ... je. 7 Herinner ... je. 8 bemoei je. 9 vergist
zich/u. 10 Scheer ... je.

Unit 22

Exercise 22.1

1 Nee, je hoeft je kleren niet uit te trekken. 2 Nee, je hoeft geen bloedtest te doen. 3 Nee, je hoeft geen medicijnen te nemen. 4 Nee, je hoeft niet weer terug te komen. 5 Nee, je hoeft niet meteen voor het consult te betalen.

Exercise 22.2

1 ... om in de tuin te werken. 2 ... om te drinken. 3 ... om tennis te spelen. 4 ... om naar het nieuws te kijken. 5 ... om te lezen.

Exercise 22.3

1 ... om de auto te laten wassen. 2 ... om haar vriendin voor het eten uit te nodigen. 3 ... om naar nieuwe voetbalschoenen te kijken. 4 ... om haar vriendin Katja op te bellen. 5 ... om Placido Domingo te horen zingen, 6 ... om samen huiswerk te maken.

Exercise 22.4

1 Nee, ik moet nog huiswerk maken. 2 Nee, ik wil vanavond niet naar de voetbalwedstrijd kijken. 3 Nee, ik kan je niet met wiskunde helpen. 4 Ja, ik blijf vanavond thuis eten. 5 Nee, ik kom beneden koffie drinken.

Exercise 22.5

1 Karin heeft een vriendin proberen te bellen/Karin heeft geprobeerd, een vriendin te bellen. 2 Johan is Peter met zijn wiskunde komen helpen. 3 Johan is bij de Beumers blijven eten. 4 Erik heeft de krant zitten (te) lezen. 5 Sanne heeft Erik de aardappels laten schillen.

Exercise 22.6

1 Sanne kan de buurman horen zingen. 2 Erik moet de accu van de auto laten opladen. 3 Karin wil vanavond bij een vriendin blijven eten. 4 Peter mag bij de rector over een probleem komen praten. 5 Erik wil morgenochtend met een vriend gaan vissen.

Unit 23

Exercise 23.1

1 Erik gaat vandaag met Sanne naar de markt. 2 Erik eet elke zaterdag
bij visboer Stegeman een haring./Erik eet elke zaterdag een haring bij visboer Stegeman. 3 Sanne vraagt de groenteman wat de aardbeien kosten.
4 Sanne heeft zin om een kop koffie te drinken. 5 Erik moet om twaalf
uur bij de kapper zijn.

Exercise 23.2

1 Op zaterdag speelt Peter altijd voetbal. 2 Om negen uur fietst hij met
Johan naar de voetbalclub. 3 Met de trainer doen de jongens eerst een
lange warm-up. 4 Na de warm-up spelen ze in twee teams een oefenwedstrijdje. 5 Meestal fietsen Johan en Peter rond twaalf uur weer naar huis.

Exercise 23.3

1 Toen Erik en Sanne in Parijs waren, gingen ze naar het Louvre. 2 Ze
aten veel croissants en ze dronken de beste café au lait. 3 Ze gingen naar
Montmartre, maar het weer was slecht op die dag. 4 Sanne wilde naar de
Eiffeltoren, omdat ze panoramafoto's wilde maken. 5 Sanne maakte
foto's, terwijl Erik met een andere Nederlandse toerist praatte.

Exercise 23.4

1 Hij zegt dat het weer bijna altijd goed is. 2 Hij zegt dat het heel druk
was in het Louvre/Hij zegt dat het heel druk in het Louvre was. 3 Hij zegt
dat mama fantastische foto's maakt. 4 Hij vraagt hoe het thuis gaat. 5 Hij
vraagt of we twee keer per dag met de hond lopen.

Unit 24

Exercise 24.1

1 die. 2 dat. 3 wie. 4 waarvoor. 5 die.

Exercise 24.2

1 fout. 2 goed. 3 fout. 4 goed. 5 goed.

Exercise 24.3

1 die. 2 dat. 3 wat. 4 die. 5 wie. 6 die. 7 die. 8 wat. 9 die. 10 dat.

Exercise 24.4

1 die naast Marco zit. 2 met wie Kees altijd tennis speelt. 3 dat totaal slecht geblondeerd is. 4 die altijd met Elly zit te flirten. 5 wat ik echt niet snap.

Exercise 24.5

1 waarin ze haar notities schreef/waar ze haar notities in schreef. 2 waarachter een trap zat/waar een trap achter zat. 3 waarmee Anne haar kamer gezellig maakte/waar Anne haar kamer gezellig mee maakte. 4 aan wie Anne een grote hekel had. 5 van wie Anne heel veel leerde.

Unit 25

Exercise 25.1

1 bij/naast. 2 in. 3 aan. 4 onder. 5 op. 6 naast. 7 boven. 8 tussen. 9 onder/bij. 10 achter/bij.

Exercise 25.2

1 naar. 2 naar. 3 op. 4 met. 5 naar. 6 tot. 7 langs. 8 naar. 9 bij. 10 in.

Exercise 25.3

1 in, op. 2 op, om. 3 Tussen. 4 Onder/Tijdens. 5 over. 6 voor, over. 7 rond/tegen. 8 per, op. 9 In. 10 van, tot.

Exercise 25.4

1 naar . . . toe. 2 tegen . . . aan. 3 met . . . mee. 4 achter . . . aan. 5 onder . . . door. 6 op . . . af. 7 door . . . heen. 8 tussen . . . door.

Exercise 25.5

1 op. 2 af. 3 over. 4 uit. 5 langs. 6 voorbij.

INDEX

Page numbers in **bold** refer to detailed discussions